MW00638388

Spring of Water International Ministries has added an option of viewing the Bible study video online. Please follow the steps listed below, register online at our website, then enter the following code.

**9kgQiV0gxzEd5wS**

After following each step, then you can view the video part of the study guide on your computer, cell phone, or tablet.

## Instruction for initial registration for viewing online Bible study video:

1) Open the browser and go to Spring of Water International Ministries website at www.sowim. org
2) Click on "Online Viewing Signup" at the top right corner of the webpage.
3) On the new page that popped up, enter your "Username", "Password", and "Email address", then click "Register".
4) You will receive a confirmation email from SOWIM. Please click on the link in the message to activate your account.
5) Go to the homepage at www.sowim.org and click "Online Viewing Login" at the top right corner of the webpage.
6) On the new page that popped up, enter your "Username" and "Password", then click "Login".
7) It will direct you to the "Online Material" page. Please enter the serial number provided in this manual inside the "Enter Code" window, then click "Submit". You would then be able to view the video you have purchased.
 * Note: This code can only be used once, it cannot be shared with other individuals. If you have any questions, please contact us at info@sowim.org.

## Instruction for viewing online Bible study video with prior registration:

1) Open the browser and go to the Spring of Water International Ministries website at www. sowim.org
2) Click on "Online Viewing Login" at the top right corner of the webpage.
3) On the new page that popped up, enter your "Username" and "Password", then click "Login".
4) Once you are logged in, you will have access to all the videos in your account.

SPRING OF WATER INTERNATIONAL MINISTRIES
THE BOOK OF NEHEMIAH STUDY GUIDE

# The Book of
# Nehemiah Study Guide

ENGLISH

English Edition

# Table of Contents
# The Book of Nehemiah

# Preface

Among all Biblical figures, Nehemiah clearly stands out in his bold, passionate, and righteous character. As we study Nehemiah through SOW 's Book of Nehemiah Overview, not only are we drawn by Nehemiah's stamina and charisma as a leader, we are also encouraged by his faithful prayers and self-less posture. Indeed, generations of Christians in history have been impacted by Nehemiah's example of what it looks like to truly trust in God and serve Him.

This Bible study set on Nehemiah is the second episode of "The Overview of Ezra & Nehemiah". From the videos, readers have a chance to see a rich selection of museum relics. Most notably, readers will see the remains of the walls of Jerusalem, discovered by archaeologists in 2007, which Nehemiah had built at the time of Persian rule. The systematic Bible study and discussion questions presented in each chapter allow all readers (across contexts such as Sunday School and small group Bible study) to deepen their understanding of the Book of Nehemiah and experience the flow of events as if they were actually there.

Praise the Lord for raising up many SOWing Warriors in Hong Kong, North America, Taiwan, and other countries in Asia who have offered financial support for the production of

Nehemiah. God has also called many brothers and sisters in Christ to offer their time to serve as volunteer translators, readers, and copy editors for the text material. It is through the unity and teamwork of this family in Christ that enabled the Book of Nehemiah Study Guide to come to fruition. Together with previously published Book of Esther Study Guide and Book of Ezra Study Guide, Book of Nehemiah Study Guide completes SOW's Bible study series to allow brothers and sisters in Christ to enjoy an in-depth study of Jewish post-exilic history.

Our collective prayer is for the Word of God to be taught and shared around the world for the spiritual nourishment of God's children. At the same time, we want to see the truth of the Bible spread to all corners of the world through missionary effort for the salvation of lost souls - "so that it yields seed for the sower and bread for the eater!"

Rev. Susan Chen

Founder and lifetime volunteer,
Spring of Water International Ministries (SOW)
California, USA

# Foreword

    Spring of Water International Ministry Multimedia Bible Study Set (SBSS) is a learning package specially made for Bible study. Based on Bible content, we retain expert opinion from reputable Bible scholars, and we dispatch professional filming teams to biblical historical sites to produce this teaching material in video and print forms. We then design the curriculum following the 'Open Learning" principle in spirit and "Media-Based instruction" model in form. The 'open learning' principle allows the teacher to break away from traditional one-way, verbal teaching. Class participation through questions and discussion is strongly encouraged here. The use of multimedia material illustrates the Bible content through the presentation of archaeological finds, on-site explanation, succinct graphics and tables, and 2D/3D computer animation to inspire active participation in learning.

    Although this combination may not be the ONLY method of effective teaching, it does receive many favorable responses from Bible study groups in various Bible studying situations. The use of SBSS may increase Sunday school attendance, enhance learning, and share in small group Bible studies. Students may gain deeper understanding after viewing the video.

The participation in the discussion, and sharing personally within the small group also contribute to the better appreciation of the Bible and its implications for everyday life.

The exact process of how to use this SBSS in the most effective way can be found in the Appendix section of this book.

In places that lack teachers or ministers, SBSS can provide high-quality Bible study materials with sound theology. It has a comprehensive teaching plan for each lesson. This alleviates the burden and pressure of teachers preparing for the Bible study class. Using SBSS makes it easier for brothers and sisters to learn how to lead a Sunday school class or a small group Bible study. It can be brought to the mission fields, as a tangible tool to train local co-workers. SBSS can also be used as an ideal supplemental audio/video teaching material for sermons or seminary classes, rendering the history, geography, and artifacts described in the Bible visible and personable, much more than printed words alone can do.

To all our users, feel free to select and adjust the procedures suggested in the Appendix. Our mission is to continue to produce a complete multimedia Bible study material that can help and equip churches, as well as Christian brothers and sisters to read, examine, and study the Bible better than ever before. We welcome your feedback. You may reach us at www. sowim.org. Thank you very much!

# Lesson 1
# The Prayer of Nehemiah
# (Nehemiah 1:1-11)

## I. Scripture Reading

Nehemiah 1:1-11

## II. Synopsis

### 1. The Disaster in Jerusalem (Neh 1:1-4)

In the Book of Nehemiah, we often see Nehemiah expressing himself in the first person; several passages in the Book of Nehemiah are considered part of the memoir written by Nehemiah at an earlier time. In Hebrew, "Nehemiah" means "the Lord is comfort" or "the Lord has mercy". Since "Nehemiah" was a common name at the time appearing also in Ezra 2:2, and Nehemiah 3:16 and 7:7, the book begins with "The words of Nehemiah the son of Hacaliah" (1:1a), in order to distinguish this Nehemiah from the others.

The beginning Scriptures tell us that the incidents recorded in this book started in the 20th year of King Artaxerxes (446 B.C.) in the month of Chislev—the 9th month of the Jewish calendar, sometime between November and December. Nehemiah was serving in the palace in Susa, far away from Jerusalem. When he heard from his brother Hanani that "The survivors there in the province who escaped captivity are in great trouble and shame; the wall of Jerusalem is broken down, and its gates have been destroyed by fire" (1:3), he was deeply grieved. Although Nehemiah enjoyed great wealth and status as a high-ranking official in King Artaxerxes' empire, he broke down and wept at the news. He mourned for days, fasting and praying over the disaster that had befallen his hometown (1:4).

This reference to the walls of Jerusalem being destroyed and the gates burned is not the same as the disaster brought on by the Babylonian army under King Nebuchadnezzar when they captured Jerusalem in 586 B.C., which happened more than 100 years before the time of Nehemiah. Rather, the destruction and burning cited here are probably related to the events in Ezra 4:7-24, where the local rulers and leaders accused the Jews before King Artaxerxes and attacked Jerusalem, set the gates on fire, destroyed the walls, and halting its rebuilding by force.

## 2. Nehemiah Prayed and Confessed (Neh 1:5-7)

Even though Nehemiah was living a privileged life in the palace, he was a God-fearing man who had not forgotten his homeland. Upon receiving the terrible news of the broken walls and burned gates in Jerusalem, he immediately prayed to God. He recognized that in order to reverse the fate of Israel, he must fully rely on the Lord and pray! Nehemiah's prayers demonstrate his knowledge of God's attributes, the relationship between God and the Jews, his reverence of the law that God gave to Israel through Moses, and his belief that the Jews suffered subjugation, misery, and exile because they had sinned and turned away from God.

From Nehemiah's proclamation in his prayers, "the God of heaven, the great and awesome God" (1:5), this God is not just the God of Israel, but the Creator of heaven and earth. Nehemiah believes that the God of heaven and earth is the Almighty God who has the power to save the Israelites, those who had escaped the captivity (1:2) and had lost their homeland. Had not "the great and awesome"

God moved King Cyrus to decree that the exiled Jews should return to Jerusalem and rebuild the temple a hundred years ago? Nehemiah trusts that his God is the God who "keeps covenant and steadfast love" (1:5) with His people forever.

However, the Israelites failed to follow God's commandments, laws, and ordinances. Therefore, in his prayer, Nehemiah confessed to God, "We have sinned against you. Both I and my family have sinned" (1:6). Although Nehemiah himself had not forsaken God's word, Nehemiah used "we" instead of "they." Despite being a high official in the palace and having remained faithful to God, he humbly identified himself with the rest of the Israelites.

## 3. Nehemiah Prayed for the Lord's Mercy (Neh 1:8-11)

Nehemiah often cited Scripture from Deuteronomy in his prayers. Apparently, he had taken God's commandments, statutes, and ordinances to heart. He knew well that if the people of Israel were unfaithful to God, God would "scatter them among the peoples," but if they returned to God and kept His commandments, God would gather them from the farthest corners and bring them back to the holy city that He had chosen for them. In II Chronicles 6:4-6, King Solomon prayed after building the temple,

"Blessed be the Lord, the God of Israel, who with his hand has fulfilled what he promised with his mouth to my father David, saying, 'Since the day that I brought my people out of the land of Egypt, I have not chosen a city from any of the tribes of Israel in which to build a house, so that my name might be there, and I chose no one as ruler over my people Israel; but I have chosen Jerusalem in order that my name may be there, and I have chosen David to be over my people Israel.'" Nehemiah's prayer in verse 10 is almost identical to that in Deuteronomy 9:29. Having grown up in captivity, Nehemiah was not required to study God's Word to fulfill his job function. His deep knowledge of God's Word must have come from his love for God rather than out of obligation. His in-depth knowledge of Scripture is indeed a good example for us to follow.

Nehemiah was deeply aware of the eternal covenant between God and Israel—that He is their Lord and Father and they are His servants and His people. Nehemiah acknowledged that God "redeemed the people of Israel by His great power and His strong hand" (1:10). God performed many signs and wonders, leading them out of the misery that they endured under the Pharaohs and into the promised land of Canaan (around 1446 B.C.). Nehemiah proclaimed in his prayer that the eternal covenant between God and the people of Israel did not only stand during Moses' generation, but was intended to endure forever.

Therefore, he believed that God would definitely save His people from being persecuted by their enemies in Jerusalem.

Finally, in verse 11, Nehemiah prayed specifically for the redemption and deliverance of the Israelites. He prayed: "O Lord, let your ear be attentive to the prayer of your servant, and to the prayer of your servants who delight in revering your name." Although he knew that King Artaxerxes was the king of the empire, he also knew that the king was merely a man, and that only the great and awesome God has the ultimate control of everything. He prayed to God, "Give success to your servant today, and grant him mercy in the sight of this man!" It is clear that he had been praying and fasting and actively seeking God's help for Jerusalem's plight for many days. His faith came from knowing and trusting in God's faithfulness and believing that He would honor His covenant with the people of Israel in the face of their current troubles. It is written in Hebrews 4:16, "Let us therefore approach the throne of grace with boldness, so that we may receive mercy and find grace to help in time of need," and this is precisely what Nehemiah did.

## III. Video Viewing

Play DVD Section, "Outline of Ezra-Nehemiah Introduction

and the Stages of the Third Return," and Section, "The Prayer of Nehemiah."

## IV. Study Questions

### 1. Fill in the blank

(1) The words of _____ the son of Hacaliah. In the month of Chislev, in the twentieth year, while I was in _____ the capital. (Nehemiah 1:1)

(2) The survivors there in the province who escaped captivity are in great trouble and shame; the wall of _____ is broken down, and its gates have been destroyed by fire. (Nehemiah 1:3)

(3) O Lord God of _____ , the _____ God, who _____ with those who love him and keep his commandments. (Nehemiah 1:5)

(4) The reigning king at the time of Nehemiah was King Artaxerxes (also referred to by historians as Artaxerxes I.) He ruled in the period of _____ - _____ B.C.

### 2. Scripture study

(1) In addition to *The Book of Nehemiah*, are there any other books in the Bible that also start with "the son of someone" as a way of introducing the author?

(2) What year did Ezra return to Jerusalem during the rule of

King Artaxerxes? How many years had elapsed since the time given in Nehemiah Chapter 1?

(3) Find the similarity between Nehemiah's prayer in Nehemiah 1:8-9 and the passages in Deuteronomy 4:27, 28:64, and 30:4.

## 3. Discussion and sharing

(1) In Nehemiah 1:5, Nehemiah prayed that God kept His covenant of love with those who loved Him and obeyed His commands. What was the covenant between God and the Israelites?

<br><br><br><br><br><br>

(2) What are some key points that we can learn from Nehemiah's prayer?

<br><br><br><br>

........................................................................

........................................................................

(3) Please share your views of the differences and similarities between Nehemiah's prayer (Nehemiah 1:5-11) and
Ezra's prayer (Ezra 9:6-15).

........................................................................

........................................................................

........................................................................

........................................................................

........................................................................

........................................................................

........................................................................

Bible Study Process for Bible Study Group or Sunday School

This part supplies reference for group leaders and Sunday school teachers. If needed, please refer to Appendix: "Instruction for Bible Study Group Leaders and Instructors". Please feel free to adjust the process according to time limits.

## A. Preparation (5-15 minutes)

### 1. Icebreaker

Game: "My Memories"

The rules:

Starting with the small group leader, everyone takes turns introducing themselves with 1) their name, 2) their job/occupation, 3) one meaningful event they'd like to preserve in their memory and why.

• Discover and discuss the common topics and themes that emerge as students contribute different memories to the discussion.

## 2. Introduction

Events that are recorded in personal memories are preserved because they must be important to the person. Although the Bible is mostly written in the third person, memories narrated in the first person appear as well, such as in the Book of Nehemiah. By studying this book, we read Nehemiah's memoirs and learn from all the events that are meaningful to him.

## 3. Opening Prayer

Dear Heavenly Father, as we get together and study your words, please be with us and bless us. May the Holy Spirit prepare our hearts and help us to understand your words. May you open our ears so that we can know your will, follow your lead and be blessed by you. Please give us wisdom and strength through your words, so that we can live a life that is pleasing to you. We also want to seek after your heart and be a blessing to the people around us. We pray all these in Jesus' name. Amen.

## B. Development (40-90 minutes)

### I. Scripture Reading
Nehemiah 1:1-11.

### II. Synopsis
1. The Disaster in Jerusalem (1:1-4)
2. Nehemiah Prayed and Confessed (1:5-7)
3. Nehemiah Prayed for the Lord's Mercy (1:8-11)

### III. Video Viewing
Play DVD Section, "Outline of Ezra-Nehemiah Introduction and the Stages of the Third Return," and Section, "The Prayer of Nehemiah." Students watch the video and take notes.

### IV. Study Questions
Fill in the blanks: Questions (1) – (4)
Scripture study: Questions (1) – (3)
Discussion and sharing: Questions (1) – (3)

## C. Conclusion (5-15 minutes)

### 1. Summary

Though Nehemiah worked in the palace of Susa, the devastating situation in Jerusalem burdened him. Nehemiah was a God-fearing man who knew God and cared about what concerned God—the people of Israel. He prayed humbly for God's forgiveness of the sins that he and the Israelites had committed. This prayer in Chapter 1 was the catalyst for all the events recorded in *The Book of Nehemiah*.

### 2. Homework Assignment

Ask small group members to pray for the salvation of a friend or a family member. Small group members can write it down or print it on a piece of paper, place it inside their Bible, and recite it every day.

## ❋ Closing Prayer: ❋

Dear Heavenly Father, you are the God of heaven and earth, the great and awesome God. You keep your covenant by showing mercy to those who love you and obey your words. We are full of thanks for how you listen to us and answer our prayers. Please lead us into a deeper and more intimate relationship with you when we read your words and pray to your every day. In Jesus' name we pray. Amen!

# Lesson 2
# Inspecting the Walls Upon Being Called Back to Jerusalem (Nehemiah 2:1-20)

## I. Scripture Reading

Nehemiah 2:1-20

## II. Synopsis

### 1. The Favor of the King (2:1-6)

As the royal cupbearer, Nehemiah waited on King Artaxerxes every day, tasting not only wine for the king, but making sure that all was safe for the king's meals and lodging, a job that required much prudent care and attention. Apart from the princes, if they were present, a cupbearer was the official who stood closest by the side of the king. It was God's wonderful plan to place Nehemiah in this position.

Based on what we read in Nehemiah Chapter 1, Nehemiah had been waiting for more than four months since he prayed with a broken and contrite heart. Finally, in the month of Nisan, in the twentieth year of King Artaxerxes, God opened a window in His time. When Nehemiah served the wine to King Artaxerxes, the King noticed Nehemiah's sadness. The King asked Nehemiah: "Why is your face sad, since you are not sick? This can only be sadness of the heart." Though Nehemiah was afraid when the king noticed his sadness, he had the courage to tell the king about the ruins in Jerusalem. Nehemiah knew that King Artaxerxes had earlier ordered that the rebuilding of Jerusalem be stopped. He replied by referring to Jerusalem as "the place of my ancestors' graves". Thus, Nehemiah strategically avoided over mentioning this politically sensitive city, but instead expressed his sadness through the longing for his forefathers.

As expected, King Artaxerxes was moved by God and had compassion toward Nehemiah. The king then asked him, "What do you request?" Nehemiah prayed quietly to God before giving his answer. In the Book of Nehemiah, we find that Nehemiah prays earnestly before doing anything. Even when he was giving an answer to

King Artaxerxes, he kept praying silently to God for guidance and the proper words. After his prayer, Nehemiah asked King Artaxerxes to send him as the king's envoy to be the governor of the province of Judah (5:14) to rebuild the city of Jerusalem. Being in a good mood given the queen's presence, King Artaxerxes granted Nenemiant's request immediately. Nehemiah's life of prayer sets a good example for us all.

## 2. Return Upon King's Decree (2:7-10)

First, Nehemiah requested King Artaxerxes to give him a letter instructing the governors of the Trans-Euphrates to let him pass through their territories, to give him protection, and to supply all his needs on the journey. Secondly, he asked King Artaxerxes to issue another letter to acquire timber for the rebuilding work in Jerusalem. Not only did Nehemiah request the best imperial building material, he named Asaph, "keeper of the king's forest", for its supply. This tells us that Nehemiah not only had the trust of King Artaxerxes but also good relationship with other officials.

Nehemiah presented to King Artaxerxes three retuilding projects 1) The citadel for the protection of the temple on the north side of the Temple Mount, 2) the city walls of Jerusalem, and 3) the governor's residence for him. Everything that Nehemiah asked for was granted by

King Artaxerxes at once. However, Nehemiah did not attribute the success to King Artaxerxes, for he was fully aware that "the gracious hand of my God was upon me." (2:8)

As a special envoy, Nehemiah not only had a royal letter from King Artaxerxes, but also a military escort when he travelled from Susa to Jerusalem. His journey was quite smooth when he passed through all those provinces to the west of River Euphrates. Sanballat and Tobiah were two people who were upset about Nehemiah's return to Jerusalem. Sanballat was then the governor of Samaria. He was called a "Horonite" probably because he lived in Horon of Ephraim. However, Sanballat was a Babylonian name, therefore he was not a Jew. Tobiah was an Ammonite official, maybe a governor of the Trans-Jordan. Because the Samaritans and Ammonites occupied the land of Judah after the Jewish people were taken captive, the two joined hands in opposing the plan of rebuilding Jerusalem. Their power to rule would be challenged if Jerusalem were rebuilt and controlled by the Jews once again.

## 3. The Inspection of the Walls (2:11-16)

When Nehemiah returned to Jerusalem, just as what Ezra did, he "stayed there three days." (Ezra 8:32; Nehemiah 2:11) He might have spent these three days to pray, to observe the environment, and to seek the will of God for what he should do for Jerusalem. Three days later, he set out during the night with a few men to inspect the walls of Jerusalem. Nehemiah might not have wanted others to know about the rebuilding plan before its finalization. In 2:16, he described, "the officials did not know where I had gone or what I was doing; I had not yet told the Jews, the priests, the nobles, the officials, and the rest that were to do the work." This could have been in turn, to avoid the attention of enemies and any unnecessary trouble.

Nehemiah went out through the Valley Gate located in the northwestern corner to inspect the ruins of the city walls. First, He went eastward toward the Dragon's Spring (location unknown). Next, he went southward toward the Dung Gate, which was the southernmost part of Jerusalem at the time and through which people could reach the Valley of Hinnom. Nehemiah then moved on to the Fountain Gate and the King's Pool. Many scholars think that the King's Pool might be the pool and tunnel built by King Hezekiah as recorded in 2 Kings 20:20: "he (King Hezekiah) made the pool and the conduit and brought water into the city." When Nehemiah arrived, the walls might have been severely destroyed. As written in 2:14, "there was no place for the animal I was riding to continue", so he could only go up the valley to inspect the rest of the damage done to the walls, going up from the south and re-entering Jerusalem through the Valley Gate, thus ending his inspection tour that night.

Today, in the Walls of Jerusalem National Park, the remains from a section of walls of the City of David can be clearly seen around the northeastern corner of the park. In 2007, archaeologists confirmed that this wall of approximately 30 meters was exactly the part rebuilt by Nehemiah during the ancient Persian Empire. Give thanks to our God that in the past 2,500 years, despite countless wars, this part of the wall rebuilt by Nehemiah was preserved. It bears witness to the work that Nehemiah, God's faithful servant, had accomplished for the kingdom of God with all his heart, mind, soul, and strength!

## 4. Rise Up to Rebuild (2:17-20)

Nehemiah knew when it was appropriate to talk about his plan, and to encourage the officials, nobles, and the people to unite and rebuild Jerusalem. Despite his being a special envoy of the king and the governor of Judah, Nehemiah did not harshly order the people in Jerusalem to rebuild. Instead, he humbled himself and shared their feelings of disgrace and humiliation in their troubled time. This is one of the unique characteristics of Nehemiah's leadership. What Nehemiah expressed in 2:17 was heartfelt: "You see the trouble we are in, how Jerusalem lies in ruins with its gates burned" echoing the sadness that he expressed in 1:4 about Jerusalem's persecution. To Nehemiah, the ruin of Jerusalem's walls was shameful to God's chosen people. However, experiencing "the gracious hand of my God…upon me," Nehemiah was determined to challenge the faith of the Jews, so that they could rebuild Jerusalem together.

While the Jews responded enthusiastically to Nehemiah's call to rebuild the walls, the enemies were also gathering. Besides Sanballat the Horonite and Tobiah the Ammonite, there was also Geshem, who was a tribal chief of the Northwestern Arabian region. They mocked and ridiculed the Jews, saying, "Are you rebelling against the king?" (2:19) Nehemiah knew that both he and the people were surrendering to God's will and these enemies would surely "have no share or claim or historic right in Jerusalem." (2:20) With his steadfast and unyielding faith, he replied, "The God of heaven is the one who will give us success." (2:20)

## III. Video Viewing

Play DVD section "Inspecting the Walls Upon Being Called Back to Jerusalem".

## IV. Study Questions

### 1. Fill in the blanks:

(1) Then I said to the king, "If it pleases the king, and if your servant has found favor with you, I ask that you send me to _____, to the city of _____, so that I may rebuild it." (Nehemiah 2:5)

(2) "And the king granted me what I asked, for _____ was upon me." (Nehemiah 2:8)

(3) But when Sanballat the _____ and Tobiah the _____ official, and Geshem the _____ heard of it, they mocked and ridiculed us, saying "What is this that you are doing? Are you rebelling against the king?" (Nehemiah 2:19)

(4) The scripture in Nehemiah 2:15 says "…went up by way of the valley…" This valley refers to _____.

### 2. Scripture Study

(1) How many months are there between the month of Chislev and the month of Nisan?

_____

_____

_____

_____

(2) In chapters 1 and 2 of the Book of Nehemiah, how many times did Nehemiah mention "the God of heaven?" What could be his intention for saying "the God of heaven" instead of "the Holy One of Israel"?

(3) King Artaxerxes once made an order to prohibit the rebuilding of the walls of Jerusalem. Where in the Book of Ezra can we find this record?

## 3. Discussion and Sharing

(1) Fron Nehemiah's example of praying, waiting, and taking action, what principles can we learn and apply to our everyday lives?

-------------------------------------------------

-------------------------------------------------

-------------------------------------------------

-------------------------------------------------

-------------------------------------------------

-------------------------------------------------

-------------------------------------------------

(2) When Nehemiah obtained both the letter and the permission from the king, he gave all the credit to "the gracious hand of my God!" Have you ever experienced God's gracious hand upon you? Please share freely.

-------------------------------------------------

-------------------------------------------------

-------------------------------------------------

-------------------------------------------------

-------------------------------------------------

-------------------------------------------------

-------------------------------------------------

-------------------------------------------------

(3) How did Nehemiah request the Jewish people, the nobles, and the officials in Jerusalem for the rebuilding of the city wall?

-------------------------------------------------------------

-------------------------------------------------------------

-------------------------------------------------------------

-------------------------------------------------------------

-------------------------------------------------------------

-------------------------------------------------------------

-------------------------------------------------------------

Bible Study Process for
Bible Study Group or
Sunday School

This part supplies reference for group leaders and Sunday school teachers. If needed, please refer to Appendix: "Instruction for Bible Study Group Leaders and Instructors". Please feel free to adjust the process according to time limits.

## A. Preparation (5-15 minutes)

### 1. Icebreaker

Conduct the following activities before The leader the study:

- Teacher needs two dice and a big bowl.
- Divide the class into three teams. Each team will choose two players: one is the "thrower", who would throw the dice; the other is the "walker", who would walk the steps.
- The rule of the game: Normally, each walker takes only one step forward on each turn. However, if both dice turn out to be the same number, the team members of the thrower get to shout, "Royal Sword."

Then, the walker can take 3 steps forward. The first team that moves 7 steps forward wins the game.

- Encourage the team members to cheer for the two players who represent their team.

## 2. Introduction

When we get the "Royal Sword", we can move forward faster. How much do we wish to receive such privilege in everything we do! How do we get this "Royal Sword" privilege? Is it simply by chance? In today's study, we shall learn about Nehemiah and the "Royal Sword" that he receives from God's gracious hand.

## 3. Opening Prayer

Dear Heavenly Father, as we get together and study your words, please be with us and bless us. May the Holy Spirit prepare our hearts and help us to understand your words. May you open our ears so that we can know your will, follow your lead and be blessed by you. Please give us wisdom and strength through your words, so that we can live a life that is pleasing to you. We also want to seek after your heart and be a blessing to the people around us. We pray all these in Jesus' name. Amen.

## B. Development (40-90 minutes)

### I. Scripture Reading
Nehemiah 2:1-20

### II. Synopsis
1. The Favor of the King (2:1-6)
2. Return Upon Calling to the King's Decree (2:7-10)
3. The Inspection of the Walls (2:11-16)
4. Rise Up to Rebuild (2:17-20)

### III. Video Viewing
Play DVD section "Inspecting the Walls Upon Being Called Back to Jerusalem". Students watch the video and take notes.

### IV. Study Questions
1. Fill in the blanks: Questions (1) – (4)
2. Scripture study: Questions (1) – (3)
3. Discussion and sharing: Questions (1) – (3)

## C. Conclusion (5-15 minutes)

### 1. Summary

In response to Nehemiah's prayer, God miraculously moved the heart of King Artaxerxes to allow Nehemiah to return to Jerusalem as the governor of the province of Judah. However, God also allowed the enemies of the Jews to mock and threaten Nehemiah's mission. While facing the enemy's opposition, Nehemiah's faith shone. His confidence in God and his strong faith encouraged the people of Jerusalem to join him in rebuilding the walls of Jerusalem. God's gracious hand never left Nehemiah!

### 2. Homework Assignment

Remind and encourage students to continue their prayers from last week. Students can write down any opposition or difficulties that they encountered. Do not be discouraged, for the gracious hand of God will lead us!

## ✳ Closing Prayer: ✳

Dear Heavenly Father, you are the Lord in charge of all the circumstances around us. May your gracious hand be with us and give us strength to face opposition and fulfill your calling in our lives. In Jesus' name, we pray. Amen!

## Lesson 3
# Dividing the Work in Sections; Building the Walls Simultaneously in Unity
### (Nehemiah 3:1-32)

## I. Scripture Reading

Nehemiah 3:1-32

## II. Synopsis

### 1. Reconstruction in Sections

By now, the walls of Jerusalem had been destroyed for more than one hundred and forty years since the city was captured by the Babylonian army in 586 B.C. Nehemiah was not only a God-fearing man, but one who understood God's plan for His people and was willing to act on it. During the entire process of rebuilding the city wall, we see Nehemiah as an extraordinary leader. He received support from the Israelites and led them to work together to complete the reconstruction of the walls of Jerusalem. Despite his leadership role, Nehemiah did not take sole credit for completing the project. On the contrary, he generously gave credit to all who participated in this work, citing their names and the individual contributions to the rebuilding.

In Nehemiah 3, the broken walls were divided into forty-five sections. The rebuilding work began in a counter-clockwise manner, starting from the northeastern corner of the Sheep Gate. Nehemiah recorded the names of the workers, their families or their hometowns, and occasionally also provided details of each family's contributions to the construction. Nehemiah documented the names of the ten gates and described how they laid the beams and set up the doors, bolts, and bars. Even if readers may not be into all the construction details (e.g., names of the family, places, and the various gates), this chapter is still a very important piece of history recorded in the Old Testament. Although the names of some places have not been precisely determined geographically, it has still been useful to show the landscape of the city of Jerusalem walls during the Persian Empire. Today, archaeologists continue to study the Book of Nehemiah and have gradually excavated more ruins from the ancient city walls of Jerusalem. Some of the ruins have proven to be part of the east city wall in Nehemiah's time. Being about 5 meters thick and much higher than the old city walls, it was quite a massive rebuilding project.

As recorded later in Nehemiah 6:15, the wall was completed in the month of Elul. "Elul" is the sixth month in the Jewish calendar. It spans August and September in the Gregorian calendar. It means that the wall was built from about late July to mid-September of the Gregorian calendar. In the Mediterranean climate zone, summers in Jesusalem are dry, with the sun in full blast every day from a cloudless sky. Outdoor temperatures can be as high as 40 degrees Celsius or even higher. One can imagine how difficult and torturing the construction work was.

Following Nehemiah's return to Jerusalem from Susa, he quickly designed a plan for completing the wall-rebuilding project. He appointed supervisors for each section of the wall. He also carefully monitored the progress of each segment, dispatched construction materials and the workers' food supplies, and coordinated other logistics. Even though his brother Hanani might have made some helpful preparation in advance of Nehemiah's return, Nehemiah was clearly very decisive and efficient in implementing this project. Although the entire construction project involved more than forty separate segments, all of them were built simultaneously. Even though, from today's standpoint, Nehemiah had to coordinate complex logistics and personnel deployment, Nehemiah was able to lead his people to work together in an orderly and systematic fashion to complete the construction of the wall in a very short amount of time. His outstanding management abilities were indeed commendable.

## 2. Construction of the Northern and Western Walls (3:1-15)

The recording of the construction project began when the high priest Eliashib initiated his work with his fellow priests to rebuild the wall starting at the northeastern corner of the Sheep Gate, and continued as far as the Tower of Hananel. There was special meaning for Nehemiah to start the whole construction project from Sheep Gate until the Tower of Hananel, the entrance to the Temple, because it fulfilled God's promise in Jeremiah 31:38, "The days are surely coming, says the Lord, when the city shall be rebuilt for the Lord from the tower of Hananel to the Corner Gate". Nehemiah 3:1 further records that the Israelites "consecrated it (the Sheep Gate) and set up its doors; they consecrated it …as far as the Tower of Hananel." The Sheep Gate was a symbol of man's repentance and the desire to bring sacrifice to God. During the rebuilding of the Tower of Hananel, the grace of God's forgiveness was confirmed and His promise to Israel was fulfilled. Clearly, reconstructing the walls was not only a civil engineering endeavor, but also represented a renewal of promise and restoration of covenant between the Israelites and their God. The Sheep Gate marks both the beginning and the end of the project. When the high priest consecrated the "gate" and set up its doors, it represented Israelites intent to "sanctify" each and every section of the walls and gates as an offering to God.

While recording the reconstruction of the walls, Nehemiah made frequent references to those who were involved in the project. For example, the "son of ... made repairs / built /set up ...". Therefore, it is obvious that he wanted the readers to understand how everyone was working together as a team and that the rebuilding project was a joint effort. The old and young, men and women, all came out, united with the same goal in mind, which is to rebuild the wall and gates. They came from all walks of life and backgrounds; there were goldsmiths, perfume makers, etc. (v.8). They originated from different villages, some from remote areas while others from the peripheral areas of Jerusalem. Depending on the extent of damage to the walls, some sections could be repaired, whereas other sections had to be completely rebuilt. The work chronicled in Nehemiah Chapter 3 was precisely the display of the people's response articulated in Nehemiah 2:18 where they cried out, "Let us start building!"

While all the people gathered to work in unity, a negative scene arose in Nehemiah 3:5. "Next to them the Tekoites made repairs; but their nobles would not put their shoulders to the work of their Lord." Tekoa was home to the prophet Amos and governed by Geshem the Arab (2:19) during this time. We do not know if the nobles were afraid of Geshem and thus refused to participate in the construction of the wall. What we do see is that Nehemiah did not conceal the fact that a small group of people were not willing to cooperate with him, and he truthfully recorded these facts.

## 3. Construction of the Eastern Wall (3:16-32)

Beginning in Nehemiah 3:16, the reconstruction of the city wall began toward the west, turning south, then toward the east. According to Nehemiah 2:13-14, the eastern section of the wall "had been broken down, and its gates that had been destroyed by fire. ...there was no place for the animal I was riding to continue." However, Nehemiah was determined to rebuild the walls and did not give up. Therefore, he built on top of the stone wall that was built by the Jebusites to stabilize the eastern slopes of the city wall (using a stepped-stone structure). From aerial photographs of the Jerusalem walls today, one can still see the ruins of a 30-meter long city wall located on the eastern side of the City of David at the northeastern corner of the Jerusalem Walls National Park. After much archaeological research, it was confirmed (and reported in 2007) that the wall was indeed built by Nehemiah.

In Nehemiah 3:16-32, the recording of the construction took a different form than that in the first half of Chapter 3. In the first half of the chapter, the emphasis was on the sections of the wall and gates being rebuilt. In contrast, the second half of Chapter 3 focused on the construction of residential houses, jurisdictions, and landmark buildings. Even at the old city area of Jerusalem today, it is common to see people building their houses against the city walls. We can see that Nehemiah had wisdom from God when he arranged for the families to be responsible to "repair opposite and/or beside their own house." Thus, the wall that they were responsible for repairing was also the front of their own homes. This not only saved them time getting to and from work, it also gave them a greater sense of security. Nehemiah's arrangement indeed allowed for a win-win situation.

Among the people working on the construction project were the priests Eliashib, Meremoth, Meshullam, and Hananiah. However, Baruch, the son of Zabbai, was the only one praised by Nehemiah for "zealously repairing" the city wall (3:20 NIV). Baruch did not have any high or special status, unlike the high priest Eliashib, but his dedication was noticed and recorded by Nehemiah in Old Testament history. Rebuilding the walls was not only an effort of protecting the people of Jerusalem. More significantly, it also symbolized the restoration of relationship between God and His chosen people.

Again and again in Israel's history, "the people of Israel did what was evil in the sight of the Lord" and the Lord strengthened their enemies to oppress and humiliate them. Repairing the walls and gates was as important as rebuilding the Temple because it brought the Israelites into spiritual revival and a new era of restored relationship with God.

## III. Video Viewing

Play DVD section "Divide the Work in Sections; Build the Walls Simultaneously in Unity".

## IV. Study Questions

### 1. Fill in the blanks

(1) Then the high priest _____ set out to work with his fellow priests and rebuilt the Sheep Gate. They consecrated it and set up its doors; they consecrated it as far

as the Tower of the Hundred and as far as the Tower of
_____ . (Nehemiah 3:1)

(2) Nehemiah built on top of the stone wall which was built
around 1200-1000 B.C. by the _____ , to stabilize
the eastern slopes of the city wall (using a stepped-stone
structure), and to support their castles and palaces. In II
Samuel, I Kings and I & II Chronicles, It was called
" _____ ", meaning stabilizing the stone structure of
the slope.

(3) In Nehemiah 3:8, there were goldsmiths and perfumemakers involved with the "restored Jerusalem as far as
the _____ ." According to archaeological data,
the "Broad Wall" was about 7 meters thick. The entire
section of the "Broad Wall" was originally built by
_____ of the Southern Kingdom (II Chroni-
cles 32:5). Since this area was relatively flat, the city of
Jerusalem could be defeated easily by enemies with battering rams, so they tried to make the walls thicker, and
thus named it the "Broad Wall".

(4) In Nehemiah 3:16, the Nehemiah mentioned there was
not the author of the Book of Nehemiah. He was the son
of _____ , ruler of the district of _____ ,
located in between Jerusalem and Hebron.

## 2. Scripture Study

(1) From the Bible, find the background of Eliashib, the

high priest.

---
---
---
---
---
---
---
---

(2) During the time of Nehemiah's rebuilding, there were ten gates at the Jerusalem City Walls. Find the names of the gates in Nehemiah 3.

---
---
---
---
---
---
---
---

(3) Among the people rebuilding the walls, Nehemiah assigned each group of people to be responsible for constructing one segment. Occasionally, however a few of them were put in charge of building more than one seg-

ment. Who were they?

## 3. Discussion and Sharing

(1) Nehemiah repaired the walls starting from the Sheep Gate and the Tower of Hananel. Based on Jeremiah 31:38-40 and John 10:7-9, what is the significance of the Sheep Gate and the Tower of Hananel?

(2) Nehemiah recorded detailed information about each person who participated in repairing the walls. Is any of them inspiring to you?

_____

_____

_____

_____

_____

_____

(3) The people who built and reconstructed the walls of Jerusalem came from different hometowns and walks of life, including the young and old, male and female. As a Christian, how do you feel about this kind of collaboration?

_____

_____

_____

_____

_____

_____

Bible Study Process for
Bible Study Group or
Sunday School

This part supplies reference for group leaders and Sunday school teachers. If needed, please refer to Appendix: "Instruction for Bible Study Group Leaders and Instructors". Please feel free to adjust the process according to time limits.

## A. Preparation (5-15 minutes)

### 1. Icebreaker

Play this icebreaking Game: "Counting the Stars".

Preparation: The leader prepares a few projector slides with randomly arranged shapes (square, circle, triangle, and star) in black or white on each slide. For example:

| Slide 1 | Slide 2 | Slide 3 | Slide 4 |
|---------|---------|---------|---------|
| ●★★●▲ | ★■★●▲ | ▲■★▲● | ■★●▲★ |
| ▲■■★▲ | ★●▲●★ | ★■●▲★ | ▲■★■▲ |
| ★■▲●▲ | ▲■★■▲ | ■★■▲★ | ★■▲★■ |
| ★▲★●■ | ★■▲★▲ | ★■●▲● | ●★★■● |

A. The leader the class into two teams.

B. The leader explains the rules of this game: The leader will display the slides, one at a time, to both teams for 3 seconds. Then the leader will cover the slide and ask questions, such as: how many white stars (or black triangles) are in the slide? The team that gets the correct answer first scores one point. At the end of the game, the team that scores more points is the winning team. The teacher gives each team one minute to get ready.

C. Start the game by projecting the slide and asking questions, until the last slide is displayed. When the game is over, the leader asks the winning team to share their winning strategy.

## 2. Introduction

Unity gives strength to the team and can achieve greater things beyond what an individual can do alone. Let us observe how thoughtfully Nehemiah managed his team with proper assignments to each unit.

## 3. Opening Prayer

Dear Heavenly Father, as we get together and study your words, please be with us and bless us. May the Holy Spirit prepare our hearts and help us to understand your words. May you open our ears so that we can know your will, follow your lead and be blessed by you. Please give us wisdom and strength through your words, so that we can live a life that is pleasing to you. We also want to seek after your heart and be a blessing to the people around us. We pray all these in Jesus' name. Amen.

## B. Development (40-90 minutes)

### I. Scripture Reading

Nehemiah 3:1-32.

### II. Synopsis

1. Reconstruction in Sections
2. Construction of the Northern and Western Walls (3:1-15)
3. Construction of the Eastern Wall (3:16-32)

### III. Video Viewing

Play DVD chapter "Divide the Work in Sections; Build the Walls Simultaneously in Unity". Students watch the video and take notes.

### IV. Study Questions

Depending on the amount of time at hand, the leader

can pick some or all the following questions to ask students, and provide supplemental information and appropriate answers as necessary.

1. Fill in the blanks: Questions (1) – (4)
2. Scripture study: Questions (1) – (3)
3. Discussion and sharing: Questions (1) – (3)

## C. Conclusion (5-15 minutes)

### 1. Summary

God's work is usually done collaboratively by many people. Nehemiah was burdened and saddened about the broken city walls of Jerusalem. He prayed day and night for the walls. God heard his prayers and used him to call the Jews from various walks of life to rebuild the city walls together. Since then, the history of the Israelites entered into a new era.

### 2. Homework Assignment

After learning this lesson, please write down God's response to your prayers in the last two weeks and how God has moved you to take action concerning what you have prayed.

## Closing Prayer:

Our dear Heavenly Father, we love to serve you as Nehemiah did. Please teach us not to give credit to ourselves,
but humbly know that it is your hand that has achieved
all things. We are so thankful that you have not only
saved us, but have called us to be your co-workers in
your master plan. In Jesus' name we pray, Amen!

## Lesson 4

# Fearing not the Enemies with Strong Faith
# (Nehemiah 4:1-23, Nehemiah 6:1-19)
# Rectifying Internal Conflicts and Helping
# the Poor
# (Nehemiah 5:1-19)

## I. Scripture Reading

Nehemiah 4:1-23
Nehemiah 6:1-19
Nehemiah 5:1-19

## II. Synopsis

### 1. Fearing not the Enemies with Strong Faith (Neh 4:1-23, 6:1-19)

Nehemiah Chapter 4 tells us all about the strong faith and prayers of Nehemiah when he was facing opposition from the enemies, and how he became all the more determined and courageous as he led the people to complete the building of the wall.

Sanballat and Tobiah were both very angry about the attempt to rebuild the walls of Jerusalem by the Jews. They were fully aware that the rebuilding of the walls and the gates meant the restoration of faith and national consciousness for the Jews. Therefore, their first attack was psychological: they ridiculed the Jews in order to demolish their morale. Sanballat called a military parade to threaten Nehemiah and to mock the Jews about their futile effort to seek protection by the wall. Tobiah said in an exaggerated and scoffing tone that the rebuilt walls would collapse even when a fox jumped on it. This clearly showed his contempt for the Jewish people and their faith.

Nehemiah did not hastily react to the ridicule, nor did he report it to the king. Instead, he prayed before God, telling God about the enemies' contempt and opposition to the rebuilding of the walls. This was an act rooted in his faith in God, as he knew God was the shield of the Jews, who surely would not allow His people to be humiliated and despised by their enemies. He said: "Hear, O our God, for we are despised; turn their taunt back on their own heads, and give them over as plunder in a land of captivity. Do not cover their guilt, and do not let their sin be blotted out from your sight; for they have hurled insults in the face of the builders." (Neh 4:4-5) Since God had brought the people back from captivity, Nehemiah knew that the righteous God would not be pleased with the plot to keep Jerusalem in ruins. Therefore, Nehemiah remained unwavering in his mission to lead the people to rebuild the wall.

When the walls were rebuilt to half of their height, the enemies, who were jealous of the Jews, came together for a second round of attack. This time they surrounded Jerusalem with their military forces: Samaritans in the North, Ammonites in the East, Arabs in the South, and Ashdods in the West. Faced with such a critical situation, Nehemiah continued to use prayer as his first line of defense. Meanwhile, he strengthened the guarding of the walls day and night. However, the Jews, with enemies all around them, were understandably scared. Some excused themselves by saying that they were too exhausted to continue with the work while others were afraid and kept asking Nehemiah to stay with them. As the rebuilding was carried out at over forty locations simultaneously, Nehemiah could not stay in only one location. Then Nehemiah came up with a better idea. He divided his men into two groups. While half of the men did the rebuilding work, the other half were equipped with spears, shields, bows, and armor, fully prepared for a fight. Half of the men did the work while the other half carried weapons, and everyone had swords at the ready, from dawn till night.

As the building crews were widely separated from one another and the enemies had them surrounded in all directions, the wise Nehemiah designed a warning system. He patrolled the walls with trumpeters and wherever they saw an emergency, they would blow the trumpet and people would rush there to fight the enemies. Nehemiah encouraged the officials and the rest of the people, "Rally to us wherever you hear the sound of the trumpet. Our God will fight for us." (Neh 4:20) With his outstanding leadership and military talent, he could have honored himself as a national hero, but he humbly told each and every one under his leadership that it was not Nehemiah but the mighty God in whom they trusted conquered the enemies for the Israelite people!

Seeing the failure of their military threats and the nearly finished walls, the enemies started a third round of attack. This time they aimed at Nehemiah directly. They plotted to assassinate Nehemiah in the Plain of Ono. Four times they wrote him messages, requesting him to meet with them, but Nehemiah turned down all their requests. Then they started threatening Nehemiah by brewing rumors about Nehemiah wanting to become the king in Judah and building the walls for that reason. By doing so, they thought they could force Nehemiah to come out and talk to them, and they could use this opportunity to kill him. However, to their surprise, Nehemiah appeared un-moved by the rumors. Nehemiah knew that everything was in the hand of God, therefore, his way to fight the enemies was to pray to God constantly with steadfast faith, not to waver due to any external situation. Nehemi-ah's prayer was, "But now, O God, strengthen my hands." (Neh 6:9)

However, the most distressing thing was that a few people among the Jews, out of greed, accepted bribes from Tobiah and Sanballat and betrayed Nehemiah. Fur-thermore, some leaders and respectable priests ignored Nehemiah's loyalty, honesty, and dedication, but rather wanted to disrupt his work out of their own interest or jealousy. However, regardless of what the plot was—the temptation from Shemaiah the priest, the false prophecy by Noadiah the prophetess, the lobbying effort from Me-shullam in collusion with Tobiah, his relative, or plots to trap Nehemiah in the temple, Nehemiah saw through all of them. He prayed to God once again, "Remember Tobi-ah and Sanballat, O my God, according to these things that they did" (Neh 6:14).

Nehemiah knew that although the enemies wanted to intimidate him and harm him, the righteous and just God would protect and vindicate him. As expected, the al-mighty God heard his prayer. He guided Nehemiah to stay away from the snare plotted by the enemies, and enabled him to complete the rebuilding of the walls, which had lain in ruin for one and a half centuries (from 586 B.C. to 445 B.C.), in the short span of fifty-two days. This was the most remarkable achievement in the history of Israel after returning from captivity. Nehemiah's outstanding leadership, upright character, merciful heart, fearless courage, and strong faith in God make him a good example for Christians of all generations.

## 2. Rectifying the Internal Conflicts and Helping the Poor (Neh 5:1-19)

Amid the threats of war by the enemies against Jerusalem, Nehemiah faced another critical issue: the livelihood of the poor people. They were so poor that they had to mortgage their fields, homes, and vineyards; they even had to subject their sons and daughters to slavery. Even so, they still could not get enough to buy food or to pay back loans. The worst part was that they had to pay a heavy tax to the Persian Empire. Although these might have been issues long existing among the returnees, the pressure was exacerbated by the shortage of farm workers when Nehemiah asked all those who are building the walls to remain in the city of Jerusalem, in order to complete the rebuilding in the shortest possible time, and to be prepared for the battles against the enemies. This situation further worsened the living conditions of the returnees.

The people who cried out can be divided into three groups: 1. the wage earners who labored for food, 2. the land owners who already had their land mortgaged for food or heavy taxes, 3. the poor families who were forced to sell their children as slaves due to their poor economic conditions.

Though the policy of the Persian Empire was to safeguard the peaceful coexistence of all ethnic groups, their taxation was known to be very high. During the time of King Darius, in order to levy more taxes, he even implemented decrees to have tax levied based on both the current year's harvest and the accumulation of previous years. It was indeed "a tyrannical government is fiercer than a tiger." Families with many children could neither afford to raise their children nor pay their taxes. Therefore, those children ended up in slavery. Still, the rich did not treat the sons and daughters of their fellow Israelites who were sold into slavery according to the Law of Moses and the will of God.

When Nehemiah heard the cry of the poor, seeing how the nobles and officials ignored God's laws and decrees, he was furious and was determined to confront the situation, regardless of the strong opposition. The first issue was lending money for interest. In Deuteronomy 23:20-21 and Leviticus 25:37, God commanded the Israelites through Moses that when loaning money to another

Israelite they should not charge interest. However, when the officials and nobles lent money to the poor, they charged interest so severe that they would confiscate the fields of the poor and force the poor to sell their children to pay off the debts. Honoring Moses' laws, Nehemiah denounced these nobles and officials and said, "Should you not walk in the fear of our God, to prevent the taunts of the nations our enemies?" (Neh 5:9) The fear of God teaches men to be humble and respect the laws and statutes of God, so that men would be cautious with their words and behavior, and not dare to do anything to offend God. When the people of God follow the will of God, they are blessed, and they shall become a blessing for all nations. Conversely, when the Israelites not fear God and cared only about themselves, they disobeyed the will of God and lost God's blessing. This inevitably gave the gentiles reason to taunt them, as it was the situation then.

Upon hearing what Nehemiah said and seeing his example, those nobles and officials followed his advice and exempted the monthly 1% interest, returning to the poor their fields, vineyards, olive groves, grains, new wine, and oil. They decided not only to do what Nehemiah had ordered, but swore to follow God's laws and statutes.

During the twelve years when Nehemiah served as governor of Judah, Nehemiah not only gave up all of his salary from his role as an official of the Persian Empire, but also prepared food and wine, ox, sheep, and some poultry every day at his own expense, hosting in his home about 150 Israelites, officials and people from the surrounding nations. Nehemiah did not seek praise from people for his merciful deeds, generosity, and noble character. Rather he sought to please God and abide in God's blessing. Nehemiah feared God, cared for the people, followed God's will, and was ready to suffer loss himself. He set a very good example as a great spiritual leader for us.

## III. Video Viewing

Play DVD section "Fearing not the Enemies with Strong Faith"; and section "Rectifying Internal Conflicts and Helping the Poor".

## IV. Study Questions

### 1. Fill in the blanks

(1) But when _____ and _____ and the _____ and the and the _____ heard that the repairing of the walls of Jerusalem was going forward and the gaps were beginning to be closed, they were very angry. (Nehemiah 4:7)

(2) The burden bearers carried their loads in such a way that

each labored _____ with one hand and with the other held _____ . And each of the builders had his _____ strapped at his side while he built. The man who _____ was beside me. (Nehemah 4:17-18)

(3) Moreover from the time that I was appointed to be their governor in _____ , from the twentieth year to _____ year of King Artaxerxes, twelve years, neither I nor my brothers ate the food allowance of the governor. The former governors who were before me laid heavy burdens on the people, and took food and wine from them, besides _____ of silver. Even their servants lorded it over the people. But I did not do so, because of _____ . (Nehemiah 5:14-15)

(4) So the wall was finished on the _____ of the month Elul, in _____ days. (Nehemiah 6:15)

## 2. Scripture Study

(1) Besides the famine that happened when Nehemiah served as the governor in the land of Judah, are you aware of any other famines in the land of Canaan that were recorded in the Bible?

--------------------------------------------------------

--------------------------------------------------------

--------------------------------------------------------

--------------------------------------------------------

--------------------------------------------------------

(2) In Nehemiah 4:20, Nehemiah proclaims, "Our God will fight for us." Please name one or two other similar incidents in the Bible where God fights for His people.

(3) Please summarize the Mosaic laws from Exodus 20:1-11 and Leviticus 25:39-43 concerning the proper treatment of the farm workers and domestic helpers who work for their fellow Jews.

## 3. Discussion and Sharing

(1) How should we interpret Nehemiah's prayer in Nehemiah 4:4-5?

-------------------------------------------

-------------------------------------------

-------------------------------------------

-------------------------------------------

-------------------------------------------

-------------------------------------------

(2) Are there any areas damaged by enemies in your spiritual life, like the broken city walls of Jerusalem? Have you ever heard God's "trumpet call" alerting you to be on guard against the enemies?

-------------------------------------------

-------------------------------------------

-------------------------------------------

-------------------------------------------

-------------------------------------------

-------------------------------------------

(3) In *The Book of Philippians* 2:3-5, Paul says, "Do nothing from selfish ambition or conceit, but in humility regard others as better than yourselves. Let each of you look not to your own interests, but to the interests of others. Let the same mind be in you that was in Christ Jesus." This was exactly what Nehemiah did when he was the governor in Jerusalem. Are your deeds evidence of what you claim to believe in Scripture?

Bible Study Process for
Bible Study Group or
Sunday School

This part supplies reference for group leaders and Sunday school teachers. If needed, please refer to Appendix: "Instruction for Bible Study Group Leaders and Instructors". Please feel free to adjust the process according to time limits.

## A. Preparation (5-15 minutes)

### 1. Icebreaker

Play this icebreaking game: "The Year of Jubilee"
The leader needs to prepare two bags with six note cards in each bag and write down a number, starting from 1 to 6, on each card.
Rules of the game:

- Divide the members into multiple groups with 4 people to a group.
- One representative from each team will take turns to draw a card out of each bag. When the two cards show different numbers, it is the "tax collecting year" — one of the team members will be removed

from the team, as a symbolic act of the poor selling off their children to pay tax. If both cards show 6, it is the "Jubilee Year" — all of the removed team members can re-join the team.

- If both cards show identical numbers between 1 to 5, it is a "Sabbatical Year", — one of the removed team members can re-join the team. The game can be over at any time or until one team has no member left.

- The leader can encourage members to shout, "Jubilee Year" to cheer for their own team when their representatives draw cards out of the bags.

## 2. Introduction

God has revealed an ideal economic system in the Bible. People can help each other out by making loans without interest. In the Jubilee Year the debts of the poor can be removed and the mortgaged land can be returned. In this lesson, we will see how Nehemiah bring the blessings of the Jubilee back to the people in the Judah province.

## 3. Opening Prayer

Dear Heavenly Father, as we get together and study your words, please be with us and bless us. May the Holy Spirit prepare our hearts and help us to understand your words. May you open our ears so that we can know your will, follow your lead and be blessed by you. Please give us wisdom and strength through your words, so that we can live a life that is pleasing to you. We also want to seek after your heart and be a blessing to the people around us. We pray all these in Jesus' name. Amen.

## B. Development (40-90 minutes)

Depending on the amount of time on hand, Teacher can pick some or all the following questions to ask students, and provide supplemental information and appropriate answers as necessary.

### I. Scripture Reading

Nehemiah 4:1-23, 6:1-19, and 5:1-19.

### II. Synopsis

1. Fearing not the Enemies with Strong Faith (Neh 4:1-23, 6:1-19)
2. Rectifying Internal Conflicts and Helping the Poor (Neh 5:1-19)

### III.Video Viewing

Play DVD section "Fearing not the Enemies with Strong Faith; and section "Rectifying Internal Conflicts and Helping the Poor". Students watch the video and take notes.

### IV. Study Questions

Fill in the blanks: Questions (1) – (4)

Scripture study: Questions (1) – (3)

Discussion and sharing: Questions (1) - (3)

## C. Conclusion (5-15 minutes)

### 1. Summary

Nehemiah is a person of integrity. He did not fear the threats from the enemies, nor was he moved by their mockery. He held the position of being a governor, but he did not seek any personal gain from it. He refused the salaries and released the poor from paying interest. He values the significance of eternity more than the wealth of the world. His life truly reflects his faith in God.

## 2. Homework Assignment

Please think of a kind deed, within your personal financial ability, to help out a brother or sister who is in need.

## ✳ Closing Prayer: ✳

The Lord, our God of the heavens, we want to be a Christian of integrity before you. Please use our lives to bring blessing to others. Please also help us to forgive those who attack us in word and in deed. You are our fortress and our refuge. We will trust in you all of our lives. In Jesus' name, we pray, Amen!

# Lesson 5
# Casting Lots to Settle and Guard the Holy City
# (Nehemiah 7:1-73; 11:1-12, 26)

## I. Scripture Reading

Nehemiah 7: 1-73
Nehemiah 11:1-12, 26

## II. Synopsis

### 1. Guarding Jerusalem (Neh 7:1-4)

When Nehemiah asked King Artaxerxes if he could "rebuild" Jerusalem in Nehemiah 2:5, he considered the construction of the walls as only part of the overall blueprint. The wall was a physical structure. Although it could protect Jerusalem from attacks, the city could only be rebuilt and restored to its former glory when people are willing to start moving into a city where "no houses had been built." (Neh 7:4) Therefore the primary method to ensure the city's security was to find ways to encourage people to live in Jerusalem.

Thus, Nehemiah's work entered a new stage after rebuilding the walls and setting up the gates. He started reinforcing Jerusalem's security, so that people could live safely in their homes. First, he set up guards to watch over the gates of Jerusalem. However, the armed guards were limited in number and could not watch over both the gates and the Temple simultaneously. Therefore, Nehemiah trained the Levites and the singers in the Temple to take turns to guard the gates of Jerusalem. He ordered them to guard the gates strictly, "The gates of Jerusalem are not to be opened until the sun is hot; while the gatekeepers are still standing guard, let them shut and bar the doors." (Neh 7:3) Besides ordering the guards to keep special alert, he also appointed the inhabitants of Jerusalem to guard the walls "before their own houses", in order not to leave enemies with any opportunity. Only with vigilant and courageous inhabitants on the inside and strong walls on the outside can Jerusalem be kept truly safe. Therefore, we see how great the need of guarding the city was, and yet, how only few people were willing to take up this important task.

Surrounded by dangerous enemies who were seeking opportunities to attack, Nehemiah put Hananiah, along with Hanani, in charge of Jerusalem. Nehemiah picked Hananiah not because he was "the commander of the citadel" and specialized in military affairs, but also because "he was a faithful man and feared God more than many." (Neh 7:2) Nehemiah trusted that Hananiah would be dedicated to the responsibility of guarding Jerusalem and ensuring the security of its inhabitants. Hananiah gained recognition from Nehemiah not just for his professional skill, but also for his integrity and his fear of God. How Hananiah received this promotion is a good example for Christians in the business world to follow.

## 2. Genealogical records of those who returned from exile (Neh 7:5-72)

Nehemiah might have found from old documents the genealogical records of those who had returned to Jerusalem following Zerubbabel's leadership in 538 B.C. The record started with this paragraph: "These are the people of the province who came up out of the captivity of those exiles whom King Nebuchadnezzar of Babylon had carried into exile; they returned to Jerusalem and Judah, each to his town. They came with Zerubbabel, Jeshua, Nehemiah, Azariah, Raamiah, Nahamani, Mordecai, Bilshan,

Mispereth, Bigvai, Nehum, Baanah." (Neh 7:6-7) This paragraph is significant for two reasons. First, it records the names of the people whom the King of Babylon had taken captive and who returned from exile. Secondly, it lists the names of the twelve leaders, symbolizing the return of all twelve tribes of Israel to their native land.

The Israelite families recorded here, with the exception of a few with pronunciation differences, were almost identical to the names listed in Ezra 2, thus proving the authenticity of the records. Looking more closely, the records could be divided into three parts. First, v.8-24 recorded the number of people based on family names. v. 25-38, except for v. 34 and v. 35, recorded the number of people based on the cities in which they lived. v. 39 on word recorded the families of priests as well as those serving in the Temple, including the singers, gatekeepers, the descendants of the temple servants, and the servants of Solomon. This must have been a comprehensive record because it included 642 people who could not show that their families had descended from Israel (Neh 7:62) and three families who could not prove that they were from the orthodox priesthood lineage (Neh 7:63). Thus, we see that those Israelites who returned from exile had arrived in the province of Judah with a mission of ethnic preservation and that they highly valued ancestral tradition and orthodox lineage.

The genealogical record, in Nehemiah 7:70-72, was more thorough than that in Ezra 2:69. It listed respectively all the gold, silver and bowls for the Temple, and the garments for priests that were contributed by heads of the families, the governor, and the people. The quantity of the gold and silver was quite impressive. Besides the fifty gold bowls, 41,000 darics of gold were offered. All together, it was equivalent to approximately 340 kilograms of gold. From the sincere offering, we sense how much those returning from exile cared about the worship in the Temple and how firmly they supported the rebuilding of Jerusalem. These people eagerly looked forward to the restoration of their covenant relationship with God.

## 3. Moving into Jerusalem (Neh 7:73; Neh 11:1-12:26)

The scripture passage from Nehemiah 11:1-12:26 includes a complex name list, which explains to us how Nehemiah resettled the people in Jerusalem. It shows us how the Judahites and Benjaminites were re-settled throughout the land and the number of priests and Levites serving in the Temple as well as their genealogy.

It is stated in Nehemiah 11:3, "in the towns of Judah all lived on their property in their towns: Israel, the priests, the Levites, the temple servants, and the descendants of Solomon's servants." An almost identical verse appeared in Nehemiah 7:73, "the priests, the Levites, the gatekeepers, the singers, some of the people, the temple servants, and all Israel settled in their towns." Clearly, even though the construction of walls in Jerusalem had been completed, most of the people, the priests, the Levites, the temple servants, and Solomon's servants, lived on their ancestral property in other towns and villages in the province of Judah.

After the Israelites were taken captive, many gentiles moved into Jerusalem. Their numbers were still significant before the Israelites' return. Nehemiah knew that if more Israelites could move into the city, not only the political situation but also the spiritual condition of the holy city would be improved. However, most people and temple servants were living in other towns and villages at the time. Therefore, Nehemiah's next urgent task was to move more returnees into Jerusalem because there were not many who volunteered to move. In order to be fair, Nehemiah cast lots to bring every one out of ten Israelites to live in Jerusalem' and "the people blessed all those who willingly offered to live in Jerusalem." (Neh 11:2) After Nehemiah moved one tenth of the people into Jerusalem, the holy city, which had been abandoned for 140 years, gradually revived in prosperity. God's prophecies were amazingly fulfilled in front of everyone's eyes.

Nehemiah 11:4-9 lists the genealogical records of the

Judahites and the Benjaminites. From this record, we see that the Judahites and Benjaminites, except for the temple servants, formed the main population in the holy city. This is because their ancestors supported the House of David during the kingdom split; they continued to view Jerusalem as the center for worshiping the LORD and abided in the Kingdom of Judah. The northern kingdom, on the other hand, set up two altars, lured people to worship the golden calf, and drifted farther and farther away from God. Interestingly, almost half of the cities listed in Nehemiah 11:25-29 were not in the province of Judah. Also, five cities listed in verses 34 and 35 where the Benjaminites lived were in the area near the sea, west of the province of Judah. It seemed that the author deliberately listed these cities to inform the readers that the ancestral properties of the Israelites reached beyond the mapped administrative domain of the province of Judah by the Persian Empire.

Nehemiah 12:1-26 is a continuation of the record in Nehemiah 11. The passage lists the names of the family members and tribe leaders of Levites and the high priests during the three returns. Nehemiah 12:10-11 lists the genealogy of the high priest Jeshua, thereby introducing the high priest Joiakim. Thus, the name list in Nehemiah 12:1-9 covers the period beginning with when Jeshua became high priest. The list in 12:12-21 begins when Joiakim be-

came high priest, and the list in 12:22-25 begins when
Eliashib became high priest. However, in 12:26, at the end
of the record, only Jeshua and Joiakim were mentioned
again. The name of Eliashib was replaced by Ezra the
scribe and Nehemiah the governor. It is evident that
Eliashib displeased God because he desecrated his sacred
duties (Neh 13:1-9). In Nehemiah 12:26, the scripture
says: "These were in the days of Joiakim son of Jeshua
son of Jozadak, and in the days of the governor Nehemiah
and of the priest Ezra, the scribe." This shows that every
name recorded here is indispensable, because everyone
serves an important role in this grand historical event of
returning to the Promised Land to rebuild Jerusalem.
Reading Nehemiah's genealogical records, we begin to
realize how much the Israelite returnees treasured their or-
igin of faith and valued their lineage from generation to
generation.

# III. Video Viewing

Play DVD section: "Casting Lots to Settle and Guard the
Holy City".

## 1. Fill in the blanks

(1) I said to them, "The gates of Jerusalem are not to be opened until _____ ; while _____ are still standing guard, let them shut and bar the doors." (Nehemiah 7:3)

(2) Now the leaders of the people lived in Jerusalem; and the rest of the people cast lots to bring _____ out of ten to live in the holy city Jerusalem, while ____ remained in the other towns. (Nehemiah 11:1)

(3) These were in the days of Joiakim son of Jeshua son of Jozadak, and in the days of the governor _____ and of the priest _____, the scribe. (Nehemiah 12:26)

(4) From the list provided in Nehemiah 11:4-9, we learn that the people of _____ lived in the city of Jerusalem, other than the priests and those who worked in the temple at that time.

## 2. Scripture Study

(1) What is the daric?

---

---

---

(2) Why was the number of the Levites far smaller than the number of the priests on Nehemiah's list?

(3) Are there other incidents in the Bible where people made decisions by casting lots?

## 3. Discussion and Sharing

(1) If, like Nehemiah you run short on people and resources when starting a business or working on a project like rebuilding Jerusalem, what would your attitude be and what would you do?

(2) Why did Nehemiah want the returnees to move into Jerusalem?

(3) Based on your study of *The Book of Nehemiah* so far, please list three similarities and three differences between you and Nehemiah. What are Nehemiah's strengths that are worth learning from?

-----

-----

-----

-----

-----

-----

-----

Bible Study Process for
Bible Study Group or
Sunday School

This part supplies reference for group leaders and Sunday school teachers. If needed, please refer to Appendix: "Instruction for Bible Study Group Leaders and Instructors". Please feel free to adjust the process according to time limits.

## A. Preparation (5-15 minutes)

### 1. Icebreaker

Play the icebreaking game: "The wind blows, then the rain comes."

The small group leader needs to prepare treats as rewards for the participant..

- The group leader asks all the members to form a circle with their chairs facing each other, then takes one chair away.

- Rules of the game: The game can start with "The wind blows."

  - The leader announces, "The wind blows."

  - The members ask, "Blows on what?" (Where does

the wind blow?)

- The leader can randomly answer by choosing a unique feature among the group. For example: " It blows on those who wear sandals."

- Upon hearing the answer, those who are wearing sandals must get up and run to another open chair and sit on it.

- Whoever does not find a chair to sit on leads the next round: "the rain comes."

- He/she announces: "The rain comes"

- The members ask, "Where is it raining?

- He/She can randomly answer by choosing a unique feature among the group. For example, "It rains on those who wear earrings."

- Upon hearing this, those who are wearing earrings remain seated, and those who are NOT wearing earrings have to get up and try to find a different open chair.

- The one who cannot find a chair to sit on will lead the next round of the game – "The wind blows."
  The game will continue by alternating "the wind blows" and "the rain comes," until the group leader ends the game. The ones who have not been able to find a chair and therefore have led the games will come to the leade for a treat as their reward.

## 2. Introduction

Sometimes, the Spirit of the Lord comes upon us as wind or as rain, pushing us out of our comfort zones. Though uncomfortable, it is leading us into God's plan that will bless us. In today's lesson, we are going to learn how the wind and the rain of the Holy Spirit moved Nehemiah into new territory.

## 3. Opening Prayer

Dear Heavenly Father, as we get together and study your words, please be with us and bless us. May the Holy Spirit prepare our hearts and help us to understand your words. May you open our ears so that we can know your will, follow your lead and be blessed by you. Please give us wisdom and strength through your words, so that we can live a life that is pleasing to you. We also want to seek after your heart and be a blessing to the people around us. We pray all these in Jesus' name. Amen.

## B. Development (40-90 minutes)

## I. Scripture Reading

Nehemiah 7:1-73; 11:1-12, 26.

## II. Synopsis

1. Guarding Jerusalem (Neh 7:1-4)
2. Genealogical records of those who returned from exile (Neh 7:5-72)
3. Moving into Jerusalem (Neh 7:73; Neh 11:1-12:26)

## III.Video Viewing

Play DVD section "Casting Lots to Settle and Guard the Holy City". Students watch the video and take notes.

## IV. Study Questions

1. Fill in the blanks: Questions (1) – (4)
2. Scripture study: Questions (1) – (3)
3. Discussion and sharing: Questions (1) – (3)

# C. Conclusion (5-15 minutes)

## 1. Summary

Nehemiah set a great example for us by accomplishing all his assignments with thoughtful planning and diligent execution. He achieved results that could bless the community in the long term.

## 2. Homework Assignment

The leader asks members to find a copy of the genealogy of their family from their parents or relatives to know more about their ancestors. If a written copy is not available, members can ask their parents about the lives of their grandparents or great-grandparents about the jobs they performed, places they have lived, the number of children they had, etc. Members can share their feelings and thoughts in the next class after they become more acquainted with their ancestors through this exercise.

##  Closing Prayer:

Dear Heavenly Father, it was by your wonderful and miraculous power that you brought the Israelites back to Jerusalem to settle there after their subjugation for nearly one hundred and fifty years. We want to praise you for your mercy and love, for we know that you are watching over us in the same way in every circumstance. Thankfully we pray, in Jesus' name, Amen!

# Lesson 6
# Reading of the Law, Signing the Covenant (Nehemiah 8:1-10:39)
# Dedication of the City Walls, Managing Services in the Temple (Nehemiah 12:27-47)

## I. Scripture Reading

Nehemiah 8:1-10:39
Nehemiah 12:27-47

## II. Synopsis

From Nehemiah Chapter 1 to Chapter 7, the Scriptures record in sequence how Nehemiah returned to Jerusalem with a vision and a mission to rebuild the city, how he overcame various difficulties and opposition from enemies to rebuild the walls in fifty-two days with the people and how he led the people by example and demonstrated noble character by relinquishing his salary as governor and rectifying inequality issues among the returnees. Finally, Chapter 11 records how Nehemiah moved one out of every ten Jews into Jerusalem by casting lots. Psalm 24:3-6 proclaims, "Who shall ascend the hill of the Lord? And who shall stand in his holy place? Those who have clean hands and pure hearts, who do not lift up their souls to what is false, and do not swear deceitfully. They will receive blessing from the Lord, and vindication from the God of their salvation. Such is the company of those who seek him, who seek the face of the God of Jacob." Isaiah 2:3 describes, "Many peoples shall come and say, 'Come, let us go up to the mountain of the Lord, to the house of the God of Jacob; that he may teach us his ways; and that we may walk in his paths.' For out of Zion shall go forth instruction, and the word of the Lord from Jerusalem." Nehemiah knew deep down that the rebuilding of the walls was only a physical restoration. The real "rebuild" (Neh 2:5) could happen only when the returnees worshipped Jehovah God as their only God, treasured His words, understood His laws, and repented of past transgressions.

In Nehemiah Chapter 8 and onwards, we see the scribe Ezra reading the law to the assembly. When the people understood God's words, they fasted, confessed their sins and repented, and they solemnly signed their names on an agreement with God. Finally, the dedication of the city walls of Jerusalem in Chapter 12 marked a perfect ending. Even though the time sequence of the events above is still debated by scholars, the focal point is clear: Nehemiah and Ezra together rebuilt the spiritual life of the returnees, resulting in a spiritual revival that played a key role in Jewish history. After the people were restored spiritually and renewed their covenant with God, they started rebuilding homes, restoring the prosperity of Jerusalem, and making the holy city once again the center for worshiping God.

## 1. Ezra read the law, the people kept the Feast of the Booths (Neh 8:1-18)

In Deuteronomy 31:10-13, Moses commanded the people: "Every seventh year, in the scheduled year of remission, during the Festival of Booths, when all Israel comes to appear before the Lord your God at the place that he will choose, you shall read this law before all Israel in their hearing. Assemble the people—men, women, and children, as well as the aliens residing in your towns—so that they may hear and learn to fear the Lord your God and to observe diligently all the words of this law, and so that their children, who have not known it, may hear and learn to fear the Lord your God, as long as you live in the land that you are crossing over the Jordan to possess." Therefore, the people chose to gather together on the first day of the seventh month in the square before the Water Gate in order to hear Ezra read the book of the law.

Ezra, accompanied by thirteen esteemed leaders, stood on a wooden platform made for this occasion, opened the Torah, and read to the people. Whenever Ezra blessed the Lord, all the people lifted up their hands and responded, "Amen, Amen." They also bowed their heads and worshiped the Lord with their faces to the ground. Ezra read the law earnestly and clearly, and the people listened attentively and humbly. When they heard the words of the law and the interpretation by the priests and the Levites, the people wept. (Neh 8:9) Because the people understood God's words, they repented of past sins and hungered for God's words. For seven consecutive days, they listened attentively to Ezra's reading of Scripture. We, as God's children today, ought to also examine whether our attitude is one that esteems the teaching recorded in the Bible and hunger for God's words.

After Moses led the Israelites out of Egypt, in front of the tabernacle under Mount Sinai, he proclaimed the appointed festivals of the Lord. "The Lord spoke to Moses, saying: Speak to the people of Israel, saying: On the fifteenth day of this seventh month, and lasting seven days, there shall be the festival of booths to the Lord. The first day shall be a holy convocation; you shall not work at your occupations. Seven days you shall present the Lord's offerings by fire; on the eighth day you shall observe a holy convocation and present the Lord's offerings by fire; it is a solemn assembly; you shall not work at your occupations. These are the appointed festivals of the Lord, which you shall celebrate as times of holy convocation… Now, the fifteenth day of the seventh month…you shall keep the festival of the Lord, lasting seven days; a complete rest on the first day, and a complete rest on the eighth day…You shall keep it as a festival to the Lord seven days in the year; you shall keep it in the seventh month as a statute forever throughout your generations. You shall live in booths for seven days; all that are citizens in Israel shall live in booths, so that your generations may know that I made the people of Israel live in booths when I brought them out of the land of Egypt: I am the Lord your God." (Leviticus 23:33-43) God led the Israelites during their forty years in the wilderness. Their clothes and their sandals had not worn out. (Deuteronomy 29:5) Israelites returning to their homeland from captivity was like the second exodus. When they heard the law of the Lord, remembering God's guidance, they made up their minds to obey the commandments from the Law of Moses. They made booths with branches and lived there, celebrating the Festival of Booths with great joy.

## 2. Prayer of confession and repentance (Neh 9:1-37)

After the joyful celebration of the Festival of Booths, on the twenty-fourth day of the seventh month, the people of Israel were assembled again with fasting and in sackcloth, and with dust on their heads before God. For half a day, they stood and listened to God's words, confessed their sins, and worshiped God. The priests and the Levites led the people to read a prayer as one community. This prayer of repentance, 32 verses in length, reviewed Israel's history. With humble confession and repentance, the people expressed their gratitude for God's election and abundant promises. They repented of their stiff-necked rebellion against God's guidance despite God's great patience with them. In the end, they lost their land and lamented, "Here we are, slaves to this day—slaves in the land that you gave to our ancestors to enjoy its fruit and its good gifts. Its rich yield goes to the kings whom you have set over us because of our sins; they have power also over our bodies and over our livestock at their pleasure, and we are in great distress." (Neh 9:36-37)

This prayer echoed Nehemiah's prayer in Chapter 1. Nehemiah called on the "God of heaven, the great and awesome God" (Neh 1:5). This prayer also began by proclaiming God's greatness, "You are the Lord, you alone;

you have made heaven, the heaven of heavens, with all their host, the earth and all that is on it, the seas and all that is in them. To all of them you give life, and the host of heaven worships you." (Neh 9:6) Nehemiah confessed that he, his fathers, and the Jews failed to keep the commandments, the statutes, and the ordinances that God commanded his servant Moses. (Neh 1:7) This prayer also confessed many times that "our ancestors acted presumptuously and stiffened their necks and did not obey your commandments; they refused to obey, and were not mindful of the wonders that you performed among them; but they stiffened their necks and determined to return to their slavery in Egypt." (Neh 9:16-17, 29, 34) However, God's ultimate purpose did not end with punishing their sins. Nehemiah trusted what God promised, "If you are unfaithful, I will scatter you among the peoples; but if you return to me and keep my commandments and do them, though your outcasts are under the farthest skies, I will gather them from there and bring them to the place at which I have chosen to establish my name." (Neh 1:8-9) The people also knew, "You have been just in all that has come upon us, for you have dealt faithfully and we have acted wickedly." (Neh 9:33) The people of Israel turned away from their transgressions and pleaded with God to look on their misery as slaves in captivity, for they knew that they served a "gracious and merciful" God. (Neh

9:17)

Coming back to Jerusalem, they knew "our God... (is) the great and mighty and awesome God, keeping covenant and steadfast love." (Neh 9:32) Though they repeatedly sinned against God, God still miraculously led them through an exodus-like deliverance and journey back to Jerusalem. To start a new life, they would have to rely on God's mercy, faithfulness, forgiveness, and love. This prayer deserves our meditation. Israel's history shows us a tug of war between God's good will and people's unfaithful rebellion. With genuine repentance, resolution and perseverance in obeying God's words, and trust in God's faithful, merciful, and unchanging love, we can enter into the abundant and joyful life.

## 3. Signing the covenant, obeying God's ways (Neh 9:38-10:39)

The people of Israel thought about how they followed Moses and Joshua to leave Egypt and enter into Canaan, the promised land of God. Yet, due to their sins, they were scattered and cut off from the Promised Land for more than one hundred years until now. They prayed the prayer of repentance with broken and contrite hearts, and then took an oath to "walk in God's law, which was given by Moses the servant of God, and to observe and do all the commandments of the Lord our Lord and his ordinances and his statutes." (Neh 10:29) Nehemiah the governor and Zedekiah the secretary took the lead to sign the agreement. 21 priests, 17 Levites, and 44 leaders of the people signed on behalf of all the people to start a new life according to the commandments, ordinances and statutes of the Lord.

From Nehemiah 10:30-39, we see this new life demonstrated in six ways. First, the people vowed not to intermarry with gentiles in order to avoid serving foreign gods, to preserve the Hebrew culture through their descendants, and to have faith in Jehovah God alone. This vow was the same as that recorded in Ezra Chapters 9 and 10. Second, they vowed to keep the Sabbath, not to work or trade on the Sabbath day; they also vowed to grant the remission of their neighbors' debt and set their slaves free in the Sabbath year. Third, they vowed to set apart one-third of a shekel of silver every year for the offering, the showbread and the service, and duties of the house of God. This amount was equal to about 3.5 grams or one-eighths of an ounce of silver. Fourth, the priests, the Levites or the people chosen through the casting of lots each year would be responsible for preparing the wood used for burning offerings on the altar of the Lord. Fifth, they vowed to bring the first part of their harvest and the first-born of their sons and of their livestock to the house of the Lord year after year, as it was written in the law. Sixth,

they vowed to tithe from their land to support the livelihood and service of the Levites in the Temple.

As God spoke in Exodus 19:5-6, "you shall be for me
a priestly kingdom and a holy nation," the returnees, under the leadership of Nehemiah and Ezra, vowed to start a
new life. These returnees were willing not only to conse-
crate themselves at the personal and family level, but also
to correct their social systems and business practices.
More importantly, they were willing to practice tithing to
provide for offerings and worship in the Temple as well as
the livelihood of the priests. Finally, their mutual resolution was to revive their faith, obey the Law of Moses, and
restore worship in the Temple.

## 4. Dedication of the city walls, the ministry of the priests and the Levites (Neh 12:27-47)

Nehemiah and Ezra did not celebrate the dedication
of the city walls until the people renewed their faith and
resolved to start a new life according to the teachings of
the Torah. In Nehemiah's mind, even though rebuilding
the walls of Jerusalem was important, the core mission
was to turn the people's hearts back to God. Only when
the people feared God and desired to live a sanctified
earthly life as God's people would the rebuilding of the
walls carry real significance.

To prepare for the dedication of the walls, they first sought out the Levites and the companies of the singers to bring them to Jerusalem. They used the instruments that King David made for praises "to celebrate the dedication with rejoicing, with thanksgivings and with singing, with cymbals, harps, and lyres." (Neh 12:27) The dedication of the walls was an inspiring and joyful celebration, testifying the fulfillment of God's promises. Before the dedication, "the priests and the Levites purified themselves; and they purified the people and the gates and the wall." (Neh 12:30) The priests and the Levites were instructed to purify themselves before serving in the Temple, and here they not only did that, but also purified the people and the gates and the walls before the dedication ceremony. Their prudent action showed that the grand dedication was not just a party for a finished project. Instead, it was a thanksgiving and praise offering from the people to their God.

Nehemiah 12:31-42 recorded the procession of the dedication ceremony, the route followed by each group going up the walls. According to scholarly speculation, this gathering took place at the Valley Gate on the southwest side of the walls. Officials of Judah, leaders, priests, Levites, and those who sang and gave thanks were divided into two groups: one went counter-clockwise to the right, and the other went clockwise to the left; both groups walked along the walls and met in the Temple at the end.

The priests blew the trumpets and the singers sang and played instruments. They all offered praises and thanks in one accord. As described in Nehemiah 12:43, "the women and children also rejoiced. The joy of Jerusalem was heard far away." The Jews joyfully offered their tithe for the temple, according to their vows to the Lord, so that the priests and the Levites could be well-provided and continue serving in the temple. The people's faithful offering also made possible the restoration of the ministry of the singers and the gatekeepers. Thus, the worship at the Temple was reestablished in the way it was performed in the days of King David and King Solomon. The ministry of Nehemiah and Ezra brought about a liturgy-restoring, faith-renewing, and joyous spiritual revival.

## III. Video Viewing

Play DVD section "The Stages of the Revival during the Nehemiah Period", "Reading of the Law, Signing the Covenant" and section "Dedication of the City Walls, Managing Services in the Temple".

# IV. Study Questions

## 1. Fill in the blanks

(1) All the people gathered together into _____. They told the scribe _____ to bring the book of the Law of Moses, which the Lord had given to Israel. (Nehemiah 8:1)

(2) And day by day, from the first day to the last day, _____ read from the book of the law of God. They kept the festival _____; and on the eighth day there was a solemn assembly, according to the ordinance. (Nehemiah 8:18)

(3) You are the Lord, the God who chose _____ and brought him out of Ur of the Chaldeans and gave him the name _____; and you found his heart faithful before you, and made with him a covenant to give to his descendants the land of the _____, the Hittite, the Amorite, the Perizzite, the _____, and the Girgashite; and you have fulfilled your promise, for you are righteous. (Nehemiah 9:7~8)

(4) For in the days of _____ long ago there was a leader of the singers, and there were songs of praise and thanksgiving to God. In the days of Zerubbabel and in the days of _____ all Israel gave the daily portions for the sing-

ers and the gatekeepers. They set apart that which was
for the _____ ; and the Levites set apart that which was
for the _____ . (Nehemiah 12:46-47)

## 2. Scripture Study

(1) Based on Leviticus 23:24-44, list the Jewish festivals
that occur in the seventh month of the Jewish religious
calendar.

(2) God instructed the Israelites to observe both the Sabbath
Day and the Sabbatical Year in the Law of Moses. What
is the Sabbatical Year? Please refer to Scripture recorded
in Exodus 23:10-11, Deuteronomy 15:1-3 and Leviticus
25:3-7.

(3) Which books of the Bible record the Israelites' exodus from Egypt?

................................................................................

................................................................................

................................................................................

................................................................................

................................................................................

................................................................................

## 3. Discussion and Sharing

(1) What does tithing mean to Christians?

................................................................................

................................................................................

................................................................................

................................................................................

................................................................................

................................................................................

(2) How do you address God in your prayers? Why?

................................................................................

................................................................................

........................................................................

........................................................................

........................................................................

........................................................................

........................................................................

(3) Why do Christians today no longer need to obey the
laws on sacrifices according to the Law of Moses?

........................................................................

........................................................................

........................................................................

........................................................................

........................................................................

........................................................................

........................................................................

Bible Study Process for
Bible Study Group or
Sunday School

This part supplies reference for group leaders and Sunday school teachers. If needed, please refer to Appendix: "Instruction for Bible Study Group Leaders and Instructors". Please feel free to adjust the process according to time limits.

## A. Preparation (5-15 minutes)

### 1. Icebreaker

Play the icebreaking game: "To sing songs of praise"

- The group leader selects a worship song for the class to sing.
- Divide the class into two groups and form two lines.
- When the members start singing the worship song, one line of the member moves to the right of the room and walk in the shape of a semi-circle; the other line moves toward the left of the room and walk along other half of the circle.
- Singing the worship song, members of both lines continue walking toward other line and merge back

to the original two lines.

- At the end, the group leader leads members of these two lines to face each other and clap each other's hands three times and shout "Hallelujah! Hallelujah! Hallelujah!"

## 2. Introduction

There are various ways and settings for us to express our worship and praise to God. Sometimes the worship is quiet and sometimes it is lively. It can be done either in a large crowd, or individually. In this lesson, we are going to observe a joyful, uplifting and ceremonial worship by a large crowd in unity. This is very beautiful worship.

## 3. Opening Prayer

Dear Heavenly Father, as we get together and study your words, please be with us and bless us. May the Holy Spirit prepare our hearts and help us to understand your words. May you open our ears so that we can know your will, follow your lead and be blessed by you. Please give us wisdom and strength through your words, so that we can live a life that is pleasing to you. We also want to seek after your heart and be a blessing to the people around us. We pray all these in Jesus' name. Amen.

## B. Development (40-90 minutes)

### I. Scripture Reading

Nehemiah 8:1-10:39; 12:27-47.

### II. Synopsis

1. Ezra read the law, the people kept the Feast of the Booths (Neh 8:1-18)
2. Prayer of confession and repentance (Neh 9:1-37)
3. Signing the covenant, obeying God's ways (Neh 9:38-10:39)
4. Dedication of the city walls, the ministry of the priests and the Levites (Neh 12:27-47)

### III. Video Viewing

Play DVD section "The Stages of the Revival during the Nehemiah Period", "Reading of the Law, Signing the Covenant" and section "Dedication of the City Walls, Managing Services in the Temple". Students watch the video and take notes.

#### Explain Content

The group leader explains and elaborates on the following material as time allows, while members listen and take notes.

### IV. Study Questions

1. Fill in the blanks: Questions (1) – (4)
2. Scripture study: Questions (1) – (3)
3. Discussion and sharing: Questions (1) – (3)

## C. Conclusion (5-15 minutes)

### 1. Summary

This lesson ends climactically with the dedication of the city walls of Jerusalem. We learn how Nehemiah, full of vision and mission, courageously and diligently committed to the restoration of returnees' lives and worship. His efforts resulted in the rebuilding of the city of Jerusalem and made the city the center of worship once again. Jointly, Nehemiah and Ezra led this critically important spiritual revival in the history of the Israelites.

### 2. Homework Assignment

Each member will pray before God with a quiet and yielding heart and list one teaching from the Bible that he/she commits to fully obeying. On a card, each member will write down the teaching that he/she received and his/her plan of action. Pray that God will guide you and help you to walk on the righteous path, then sign on the card. Please also bring a card to class next week. Directions will be given for how to use the card for the homework assignment in the following class.

## ✻ Closing Prayer: ✻

Dear Heavenly Father, I am full of thanks for the salvation you have given me through Jesus Christ. Please carve your words on my heart and make me pure. I want to be your beloved child, the follower of Jesus Christ for all the days of my life. In Jesus' name we pray, Amen!

# Lesson 7
# Back to Jerusalem, the Second Reform (Nehemiah 13:1-31)

## I. Scripture Reading

Nehemiah 13:1-31

## II. Synopsis

The events recorded in Nehemiah 13 took place eight years after what happened in Nehemiah 12. During this time, Nehemiah went back to Susa to report to King Artaxerxes. When Nehemiah returned to Jerusalem again, he found that, while he was not around, all of the Jews, from the priests to the leaders to the people, had forsaken their earlier vows to obey the laws of the Lord. Nehemiah 13 identifies four areas in which the Jews forsook their covenant with God: 1) the priests abused their power; 2) tithing halted; 3) the Sabbath was not observed; 4) the Jews intermarried with foreign women. Though saddened, Nehemiah courageously corrected the spiritual backsliding of the Jews and the priests with resolve. Reading Nehemiah 13 closely, we feel sorry for the Jew's backsliding in faith. Nevertheless, we admire all the more Nehemiah's heart of love for God and for the people as well as his bold and righteous character. He and Ezra deserved to be called the mighty men of God, who faithfully carried out God's will and steadfastly strove for the revival of Israel's faith in God.

## 1. The priests abused their power (Neh 13:1-9)

During the rebuilding of the walls, the high priest Eliashib worked wholeheartedly with his fellow priests and led the consecration of the walls. He was well aware that their work was to restore Jerusalem as the holy city. (Neh 3:1) Who could have imagined that, only a few years later, Eliashib himself would violate the teaching of the Torah and became an in-law of Tobiah the Ammonite? What is more, Eliashib's grandson, one of the sons of Jehoiada, married a daughter of Sanballat the Horonite. Tobiah and Sanballat were the very enemies who had repeatedly threatened the Jews and tried to destroy their efforts to rebuild the walls of Jerusalem. Instead of setting a spiritual example for the people, the high priest Eliashib ignored his God-given responsibilities and took the lead in rebelling against God's teaching.

Eliashib should have diligently managed the house of God. Instead, he misused his authority to prepare a large room in the chambers of the house of God for none other than Tobiah, a gentile from whom the Israelites were commanded to separate. During Nehemiah's first term as governor, the chambers were set apart to store offerings for the restoration of sacrifices in the Temple. "For the people of Israel and the sons of Levi shall bring the contribution of grain, wine, and oil to the storehouses where the vessels of the sanctuary are, and where the priests that minister, and the gatekeepers and the singers are. We will not neglect the house of our God." (Neh 10:39) Grossly abusing his power, Eliashib misappropriated the chambers and allowed Tobiah–a gentile–to reside in and, thus, defile the Temple.

Returning from Susa, Nehemiah noticed that Eliashib's misconduct was tolerated by other leaders. He himself therefore "threw all the household furniture of Tobiah out of the room. Then I [Nehemiah] gave orders and they cleansed the chambers, and I [Nehemiah] brought back the vessels of the house of God, with the grain offering and the frankincense." (Neh 13:8-9) Nehemiah valued and honored the holiness and the order of the house of God and was partial to no one. He did not compromise when it came to biblical principles. Such courage is exactly what today's Christians and spiritual leaders need when governing the church or facing cultural challenges.

## 2. The tithing stopped (Neh 13:10-14)

According to Numbers 18:21, the Levites' livelihood was supported by the Jews' tithing. Even though the people had vowed to tithe, their hearts soon grew cold. Ever since the tithing stopped, the chamber rooms, which had stored offerings, became occupied by Tobiah. The priest's negligence played a role in the spiritual backsliding of the society. As a result, the Levites and Temple workers, lacking their daily supply, had to work at their fields in the countryside away from the Temple.

Seeing no clergy working in the Temple and a gentile, Tobiah, dwelling there, Nehemiah furiously scolded the officials, "Why is the house of God forsaken?" (Neh 13:11) Those officials, instead of being faithful supervisors, had turned a deaf ear to such an act of rebellion against God. Nehemiah took matters into his own hand and removed Eliashib's appointment over the chamber of the house of God, and appointed "as treasurers over the storehouses the priest Shelemiah, the scribe Zadok, and

Pedaiah of the Levites, and as their assistant Hanan son of Zaccur son of Mattaniah, for they were considered faithful." (Neh 13:13) He also summoned the Levites to resume their work. Nehemiah's corrective measure obviously offended many, including the officials and the priests who acted in collusion with one another. Indignantly, Nehemiah called out to God, "Remember me, O my God, concerning this, and do not wipe out my good deeds that I have done for the house of my God and for his service." (Neh 13:14) Nehemiah made a choice to please God rather than men—a choice that was righteous and oriented towards protecting the holiness of the Temple. Even though for a time he suffered from pressure and feud from his colleagues, eventually his righteous and just acts have been praised and imitated by believers for the last 2,500 years.

The Scripture makes no mention of anyone persuading or urging the people to bring their tithe and offerings to the temple, yet "all Judah brought the tithe of the grain, wine, and oil into the storehouses." (Neh 13:12) When the people saw the prolonged corruption in the Temple being justly addressed by Nehemiah and the Levites performing their duties again, they voluntarily brought the tithe to the storehouses again. This showed that, even though the people were wrong to stop tithing, it was the abuse of power on the part of the officials and the priests that discouraged the people from tithing in the first place. This cautions us to watch out for our own attitude and deeds. Have we become the stumbling blocks to others in their journeys of faith?

## 3. The Sabbath was not observed (Neh 13:15-22)

Observing the Sabbath is one of the signs that distinguished the people of God from the gentiles. The Sabbath day should be set apart for God, so that people could spend that day reading the Bible, praying and praising God at home, as a response to God's grace. There are many teachings on the Sabbath in the Torah. However, it was indeed not easy to keep the Sabbath, as merchants would lose one day of business and the workers would not get paid. Furthermore, the majority of the residents in Jerusalem and the province of Judah at that time were gentiles, who did not have the custom of keeping the Sabbath. They traded with the Jews on the Sabbath day, just like on other days.

Yet the prophet Jeremiah warned the Israelites in Jeremiah 17:27 that one of the reasons for the desolation of Jerusalem was that the people did not keep the Sabbath holy. The prophet Ezekiel also prophesied in Ezekiel 20:23-24 that the Israelites would be scattered among the nations for not observing God's Sabbath. The Israelites had already suffered the consequences, yet they still failed to learn the lesson, rather valuing more highly one more day of income. In keeping with biblical principles, Nehemiah scolded the nobles of Judah, "What is this evil thing that you are doing, profaning the Sabbath day? Did not your ancestors act in this way, and did not our God bring all this disaster on us and on this city? Yet you bring more wrath on Israel by profaning the sabbath." (Neh 13:17-18)

To address the root cause, Nehemiah commanded that the city gates be shut and not opened until after the Sabbath, so that the gentile merchants could not enter Jerusalem to do business. He even drove away the merchants who, in the hope of sneaking in, spent the night outside Jerusalem. Also, he commanded the Levites, who could work on the Sabbath, "that they should purify themselves and come and guard the gates, to keep the sabbath day holy." (Neh 13:22) In Nehemiah's mind, the goal for observing the Sabbath was to keep that day holy. The Hebrew word "holy" has the meaning of "being set apart." According to the will of God, the Israelites were "a royal priesthood, a holy nation, God's own people". Therefore, the Sabbath was not merely a day on the calendar. To keep the Sabbath demonstrates that God's people have been set apart as priests to serve before God. God's children do not belong to this world; they are to receive God's inheritance. Such royal dignity has been bestowed to every Christian through Jesus Christ as well.

## 4. The Jews intermarried with foreign women (Neh 13:23-31)

The role of women was appreciated in the Jewish family. Women were respected and attended assemblies with their husbands. We see that when Ezra read the Torah to the Jews before the Water Gate, all the wives, with their children, were there with their husbands. (Neh 8:3) Nehemiah 10 also recorded that the Israelites vowed to obey the law of the Lord, they, "their wives, their sons, their daughters... enter into a curse and an oath...will not give our daughters to the peoples of the land or take their daughters for our sons." (Neh 10:29-30) After the dedication of the walls, Scripture tells us that "they offered great sacrifices that day and rejoiced, for God had made them rejoice with great joy; the women and children also rejoiced. The joy of Jerusalem was heard far away." (Neh 12:43) It is clear that the women were no less important than their husbands in the family. Therefore, to intermarry with gentile women stirred up a threat to the traditions and core values of the Jewish families.

Nehemiah the governor "saw Jews who had married women of Ashdod, Ammon, and Moab; and half of their children spoke the language of Ashdod, and they could not speak the language of Judah, but spoke the language of various peoples." (Neh 13:23-24) The Hebrew language was used in the prayers and the reading of the Torah. It was very important for the preservation of the Jewish culture and faith. Nehemiah worried not only about Jewish children's inability to speak Hebrew. He was even more concerned that the Israelite people would make the same mistake as King Solomon, who was lured by his foreign wives into idol worship and fell under God's wrath and punishment. Not only did the people intermarry with foreign women, but the high priest Eliashib and his family, being well aware of the teaching of Leviticus 21:14 that a priest shall only marry a virgin of his own kin, rebelled against God's words by intermarrying with the family of gentile leaders Sanballat and Tobiah. Therefore, Nehemiah chased one of the grandsons of Eliashib away from the province of Judah. He also "made them take an oath in the name of God, saying, 'You shall not give your daughters to their sons, or take their daughters for your sons or for yourselves.'" (Neh 13:25) He did this to "cleanse them (the Jews) from everything foreign." (Neh 13:30) Afterwards, he restored the duties of the priests and Levites in the Temple, and commanded the people to bring in the wood offering and the firstfruits at the appointed times. Worship was again integrated into people's daily lives, and the Temple regarded as the center of their worship.

## III. Video Viewing

Play DVD section "Back to Jerusalem, the Second Reform" and section "Conclusion".

## IV. Study Questions

### 1. Fill in the blanks

(1) When Nehemiah returned back to Jerusalem for the second time, he realized the people had abandoned their covenant with the Lord in four areas: 1) _____ abused their power; 2) _____ stopped; 3) _____ was not observed; 4) the Jews intermarried with _____.

(2) On that day they read from the book of Moses in the hearing of the people; and in it was found written that no _____ or _____ should ever enter the assembly of God, because they did not meet the Israelites with bread and water, but hired _____ against them to curse them—yet our God turned the curse into a blessing. (Nehemiah 13:1-2)

(3) ....and returned to Jerusalem. I then discovered the wrong that _____ had done on behalf of _____, preparing a room for him in the courts of the house of God. And I was very angry, and I threw all the household furniture

of _____ out of the room. Then I gave orders and they cleansed the chambers, and I brought back the _____ of the house of God, with the _____ and the _____. (Nehemiah 13:7-9)

(4). Remember this also in my favor, O my God, and spare me according to _____. (Nehemiah 13:22)

## 2. Scripture Study

(1) Please find the passage in Deuteronomy Chapter 23, where it was written that "no Ammonite or Moabite should ever enter the assembly of God" (Neh 13:1).

_____

_____

_____

_____

_____

(2) Why did Nehemiah chase one of the grandsons of Eliashib out of the province of Judah?

_____

_____

_____

_____

_____

_____

_____

(3) Please list the Scriptures from Jeremiah 17:27 and Ezekiel 20:23-24 for prophets Jeremiah and Ezekiel's warning to the Israelites about keeping the Sabbath day holy.
Defiling the Sabbath day would cause Jerusalem to be
ruined and the Israelites to be driven away from their
homeland.

-------------------------------------------------

-------------------------------------------------

-------------------------------------------------

-------------------------------------------------

-------------------------------------------------

## 3. Discussion and Sharing

(1) Nehemiah "threw all the household furniture of Tobiah
out of the room. Then I gave orders and they cleansed
the chambers" (Nehemiah 13:8-9). Did his behavior
contradict the biblical teaching to "love your enemies
and pray for those who persecute you" (Matthew 5:44)?

-------------------------------------------------

-------------------------------------------------

-------------------------------------------------

-------------------------------------------------

-------------------------------------------------

-------------------------------------------------

(2) Do you think Nehemiah matches Jesus' description of a "faithful and wise slave" in Matthew 24:45-46?

......................................................................................................

......................................................................................................

......................................................................................................

......................................................................................................

......................................................................................................

......................................................................................................

(3) Nehemiah's last prayer in the book of Nehemiah was, "Remember me, O my God, for good" (Neh 13:31). Have you ever prayed a similar prayer? If so, what were the circumstances?

......................................................................................................

......................................................................................................

......................................................................................................

......................................................................................................

......................................................................................................

......................................................................................................

......................................................................................................

This part supplies reference for group leaders and Sunday school teachers. If needed, please refer to Appendix: "Instruction for Bible Study Group Leaders and Instructors". Please feel free to adjust the process according to time limits.

## A. Preparation (5-15 minutes)

### 1. Icebreaker

Play the icebreaking game: "Simon Says".

- All the members must imitate each motion that follows the verbal instruction "Simon says".
- When a motion does not follow the verbal instruction "Simon says", members must refrain from imitating the motion.
- The leader will ask the members to stand up and face the leader. The teacher can be "Simon" or appoint one student to be "Simon" to stand in front of the members.
- The person who is Simon names and demonstrates

one action at a time, sometimes prefacing the motion with "Simon says," and sometimes not.

- The motions can be creative, with examples including: Pat your head, rub your nose, lift up your right hand…, etc.

## 2. Introduction

It is crucial for a Christian to carefully follow what the Bible teaches us to do. Often we may not be even aware of our own backsliding.

## 3. Opening Prayer

Dear Heavenly Father, as we get together and study your words, please be with us and bless us. May the Holy Spirit prepare our hearts and help us to understand your words. May you open our ears so that we can know your will, follow your lead and be blessed by you. Please give us wisdom and strength through your words, so that we can live a life that is pleasing to you. We also want to seek after your heart and be a blessing to the people around us. We pray all these in Jesus' name. Amen.

# B. Development (40-90 minutes)

## I. Scripture Reading

Nehemiah 13:1-31.

## II. Synopsis

1. The priests abused their power (Neh 13:1-9)
2. The tithing stopped (Neh 13:10-14)
3. The Sabbath was not observed (Neh 13:15-22)
4. The Jews intermarried with foreign women (Neh 13:23-31)

## III. Video Viewing

Play DVD section "Back to Jerusalem, the Second Reform" and section 11: "Conclusion".

## IV. Study Questions

1. Fill in the blanks: Questions (1) – (4)
2. Scripture study: Questions (1) – (3)
3. Discussion and sharing: Questions (1) – (3)

## C. Conclusion (5-15 minutes)

### 1. Summary

All Scripture is God-breathed. Every word, every incident, and every individual recorded in the Bible express the work of the Holy Spirit. Reading the Book of Nehemiah is like standing in front of a mirror. We learn how we can live courageously for our faith, we learn how to transform our earthly journey into one with eternal significance, and we learn how to become a blessing to the next generations!

### 2. Homework Assignment

The leader distributes a note card to each member. (Member can also use their own card, if the leader instructed them to bring a blank card in the preceding week.)

Then leader invites member to write down different ways in which they can serve their spouse (if they are married) and their friends (if they are single), and to end with their signatures. Members are encouraged to present this card to their spouses or friends, who will choose one of the services on the list.

## ✳ Closing Prayer: ✳

Dear Heavenly Father, I want to be like Nehemiah
and Ezra, serving you with a truthful heart and fearless dedication. Please hear my prayers and make me
a blessing to strengthen the faith of others! In Jesus'
name I pray, Amen!

# Lesson 8
# **Epilogue**
# **Scholar Commentaries**

## **Dr. Joseph Shao – President of Biblical Seminary of the Philippines, Manila, Philippines**

"Nehemiah was the cupbearer of King Artaxerxes. When he heard that the walls of Jerusalem were broken down and its gates burned, he felt the obligation to return. In Nehemiah 1, he immediately fasted and prayed. Why? The historical background is in Ezra 4. In the past, when explaining Nehemiah, one usually had to refer to the last chapter of 2 Kings. To be sure, that chapter mentioned the breaking down of the city walls. But more recently scholars have accepted that Ezra 4 also recorded an important part of the history in Nehemiah. This is because the same King Artaxerxes prohibited the rebuilding of Jerusalem. For this reason, the city gates were burned. Nehemiah offered up prayer to Jehovah, God of heaven, great and awesome God. He waited in quietude. There are several important theological themes in Nehemiah.

The first theme is prayer. Nehemiah chapter1 is actually a prayer of committing oneself. Nehemiah offered up prayer, asking for the grace of the Lord, that the Lord grant him a smooth return to Jerusalem. In many parts of Nehemiah 9 and particularly in Nehemiah 13, he called upon God and asked for His remembrance and grace. The prayer took the form of giving a report. I call it a celebratory prayer, as if a student says to his teacher after completing an assignment, "Teacher, I have completed it." "Oh God, may You remember me. May You be gracious!"

The second theme in Nehemiah is the theology of God's subjects, because in the 13 chapters of Nehemiah, there are many names. Nehemiah 3, on the building of the city wall, recorded the names of all those involved. In Nehemiah 8, one can find the names of coworkers who read the word of God alongside Ezra; some were leaders, others were Levites. The names in Nehemiah 7 are the same as those in Ezra 2. This is the group of first batch of returnees. Their names were listed. Why should their names be recorded? That is because, just as the prophet Jeremiah preached, they were willing to return to Jerusalem. They were willing to return to the place that God had prepared for them. In Nehemiah 10, a group signed their names, being those willing to abide by God's word. In Nehemiah 11 is recorded the names of some people who were willing to move into Jerusalem; they were willing to abide by God's word. Nehemiah 12 contains a careful record of the names of priests and Levites, those who served as leaders amongst them.

In the Book of Nehemiah, we see the importance of instruction. Ezra was a scribe. He paid much heed to God's word. He paid much attention to the Torah of the laws. In Nehemiah 8, the people were able to cautiously invite Ezra to come out and read God's word in the open square of the Water Gate. They also asked the Levites to carefully explain God's word. Nehemiah and Ezra were coworkers. Some in academia were reluctant to link the two, believing that they could not have been together. However, in Nehemiah 8 we see the name of Ezra, and in Nehemiah 12, a list shows that Ezra and Nehemiah were serving together. Today, people are generally willing to accept that the two had worked together.

In Nehemiah, we could also see that Nehemiah cared particularly about some who were weak. In that historical context, the Levites suffered setbacks amongst the ranks of God's people and were unable to take part in His work. They became weak and returned to their own fields, although the main reason was that nobody cared for their needs at the time. Hence in Nehemiah 12 and 13, Nehemiah paid particular heed to the Levites, especially those who returned to their own fields. He let them have the chance to return once again. He let them participate in celebration activities. The people welcomed the Levites to once again have the opportunity to participate in God's work. That had mainly to do with offerings, because in Nehemiah 13, while they were careless and weak, some occupied the storehouse of the temple. It was an agrarian society in those days. When there was no place to store some of the agricultural produce, such offerings decreased as a consequence. Nehemiah dealt with that matter. He let the Levites have access to their appropriate share, and encouraged these weak Levites to take part in God's work."

## Discussion and Sharing

(1) Are you inspired by the co-laboring relationship between Nehemiah and Ezra? How can their example apply to your work and church service?

(2) Do you pay attention to those who serve at your church? How do you express your care to them?

(3) When people mention your name, how do you respond? Do you like being recognized?

---

**Dr. Tremper Longman, III – Robert H. Gundry Professor of Biblical Studies at Westmont College, Santa Barbara, California, USA.**

---

"It's amazing that Nehemiah completed building the walls

in only 52 days. Indeed, the Bible presents it not as a miracle, but as an event to show that God was with Nehemiah. They're rebuilding it, and as you read the story of the rebuilding, it is exciting to see how the whole community kicks in and participates – the priests, the non-priests…Now let me also suggest that when Nehemiah learned that the enemies of the Jews, in particular Sanballat, Tobiah, and Geshem, are plotting against them and even threatening physical violence against them, that does two things: one, it takes some men off the work task as they have to protect the wall; and on the other hand, it would certainly motivate them to get that wall up fast. So, we are to see it not as a miracle but as something that is of a wonderful work of God.

How are we to look at Ezra and Nehemiah and consider their spiritual contribution? First of all, in its own time, and then, secondly, in an eschatological or future-oriented sense. First, let us remember that at the time of the Old Testament, God wanted His people to be separated. He wanted His people to stay away from the Gentiles not because God didn't care about the Gentiles. God cared about the Gentiles from the very beginning. If you go back and read Genesis 12:1-3, you see that the promise came to Abraham not just for Abraham and His descendants, but for all the families of the nations. Now the idea was that God's people would be separated. They would follow God, and they would obey Him, and God would bless them so much that the Gentiles would look at them and say,

"We want to be like them. Let us worship their God." In some sense, you can read Ezra and Nehemiah as a story of two wall buildings, not just one. In a sense the law, which Ezra comes back and re-establishes, is a law that separated Jew from Gentile, particularly in the laws concerning ritual purity, sacrifice… what we call ceremonial laws today. Additionally, there is the physical separation from the other local residents represented by the building of Nehemiah's wall. Now, in the New Testament time-period, we are told not to stay separate. But if you read the Great Commission at the end of Matthew 28, we're to go out to the nations. We are to disciple, teach, and baptize. So, this is God's plan for us today. The wall of separation has come down. We don't stay back like Ezra and Nehemiah rightly did. We go out into the nations and we proclaim the Good News of Jesus Christ. And now we are seeing, in dramatic ways, the fulfillment of the promise, that God gave Abraham that it would be a blessing that goes to the Gentiles.

An interesting fact is that Ezra and Nehemiah is one of two books – the other being Daniel – that's half written in Hebrew and half written in Aramaic. This is interesting, because at the time of Ezra and Nehemiah, Hebrew is beginning to die out as a living language and Aramaic is taking over. And so, there are a whole bunch of features of the text, which just rings true for that time period. It is interesting that the book of Ezra and Nehemiah contains two large sections that are memoirs. That is very unusual for the Old Testament. Memoirs are of course written in the first person rather than the third person. Both Ezra and Nehemiah have a memoir within it, which gives the reader a sense of "You are hearing it from a participant in the events."

Not only are Ezra and Nehemiah real people, but their personality comes across in their writings. I always find it very interesting to see just how Ezra and Nehemiah are different from each other, and how God used both personalities for His purposes. Nehemiah is kind of a goal-getter. He is kind of an extrovert. He is somebody who wants, who when he has a task, he gets it done. And when he runs into Jewish men who have divorced their wives and re-married pagan women, he goes to them. He starts yelling at them, and he starts ripping their clothes and tearing out their hair, and telling them to go back to their original wives. Ezra ran into, on a different occasion, a similar group of men. But rather than ripping their hair, he tears his own hair out, and he rips his own clothes. Sometimes, in Christian circles, we say there is only one way of leadership – I am not saying that anybody tearing out anyone's hair is the way to go today – but God could use both quiet people, or introverted people, as well as outspoken, extroverted people to accomplish His plans."

## Discussion and Sharing

(1) How did Ezra and Nehemiah positively impact the community of returnees?

(2) How does the wall of separation come down in the New Testament era?

(3) Please list the differences in leadership style between Ezra and Nehemiah.

# Suggested
# Answers

# Lesson 1: The Prayer of Nehemiah

## Suggested answers for your reference:

## ❖Fill in the blanks❖

(1) The words of <u>(Nehemiah)</u> the son of Hacaliah. In the month of Chislev, in the twentieth year, while I was in Susa the capital. (Nehemiah 1:1)

(2) The survivors there in the province who escaped captivity are in great trouble and shame; the wall of <u>(Jerusalem)</u> is broken down, and its gates have been destroyed by fire. (Nehemiah 1:3)

(3) O Lord God of <u>(heaven),</u> the <u>(great and awesome)</u> God, who <u>(keeps covenant and steadfast love)</u> with those who love him and keep his commandments. (Nehemiah 1:5)

(4) The reigning king at the time of Nehemiah was King Artaxerxes (also referred to by historians as Artaxerxes I.) He ruled in the pernod of <u>(464-424)</u> B.C..

## ❖Scripture Study❖

(1) In addition to *The Book of Nehemiah*, are there any other books in the Bible that also start with "the son of someone" as a way of introducing the author?

Suggested answer: Jeremiah 1:1— "The words of Jeremiah son of Hilkiah, of the priests who were in Anathoth in the land of Benjamin."

Ecclesiastes 1:1— "The words of the Teacher, the son of David, king in Jerusalem."

Proverbs 1:1— "The proverbs of Solomon son of David, king of Israel."

Some other authors of the Scripture such as Isaiah, Hosea, Joel, Jonah, Zephaniah, and Zechariah, also use the same style to introduce themselves, though not in the beginning of the book.

(2) What year did Ezra return to Jerusalem during the rule of King Artaxerxes? How many years had elapsed since the time given in Nehemiah Chapter 1?

Suggested answer: Ezra returned to Jerusalem in the 7th year of King Artaxerxes.

Some of the Israelites, including priests, Levites, singers, gate-keepers, and temple servants, also came to Jerusalem in the seventh year of King Artaxerxes. Ezra arrived in Jerusalem in the fifth month of the seventh year of the king (Ezra 7:7-8). There was a 13–year gap between Ezra's return to Jerusalem and the time given in Nehemiah Chapter 1.

(3) Find the similarity between Nehemiah's prayer in Nehemiah 1:8-9 and the passages in Deuteronomy 4:27, 28:64, and 30:4.

Suggested answer: In Deuteronomy 4:27 and Deuteronomy 28:64, God told the Israelites through Moses, that if they abandoned the righteous ways of the LORD and followed the Gentiles to worship their gods, "The LORD will scatter you among the peoples." However, God will never stop loving His people. Even when His people were banished from the Promised Land because of their own sins and wicked behavior, God still had mercy on them. Deuteronomy 30:4 says, "even if you have been banished to the most distant land under the heavens, from there the LORD your God will gather you and bring you back." Nehemiah's prayer is a reflection of the passages recorded in Deuteronomy. Though Nehemiah witnessed God's disciplinary acts announced by Moses, he knew he could trust God's compassion and mercy. Nehemiah prayed using God's own words, according to the faithfulness of God.

## ❖Discussion and sharing❖

(1) In Nehemiah 1:5, Nehemiah prayed that God kept His covenant of love with those who loved Him and obeyed His commands. What was the covenant between God and the Israelites?

Suggested answer: God made several covenants with the ancestors of the Israelites. For example, he made a covenant with Abraham and his descendants, one with the people of Israel (Gen 12:1-3), and another covenant with David, establishing the Davidic dynasty (2 Sam 7). According to Nehemiah's prayer, the covenant that he refers to in this prayer is The Mosaic Covenant (Exodus 19-24).

The emphasis of this covenant is on the law, and the sign of this covenant is the Sabbath. At Mt. Sinai, God told Moses (Exodus 19) that He had delivered the Israelites out of the hands of the Egyptians, broken the yoke of their slavery, and carried them out of bondage. They needed to fully obey God and keep God's covenant. God in turn blessed them to be His treasured possession and to be the kingdom of priests and a holy nation. The sign of this covenant was that they had to rest on the seventh day. On that day, they, including their servants and animals, would rest in the peace of God and be refreshed. God told them to carefully do everything He had instructed.

(2) What are some key points that we can learn from Nehemiah's prayer ?

Suggested answer: Nehemiah's prayer can be outlined as follows:

(a) Bless the Lord (1:5) - Nehemiah knew that the Lord is "the God of heaven," the "great and awesome God", and he also understood that God keeps His covenant of love and blesses His people.

(b) Confession of sins (1:6-7) - Nehemiah admitted that he and his father's house, and all the Israelites, have sinned against God.

(c) Request that the Lord remember his people (1:8-10) -
Nehemiah prayed to God with Scripture in Deuterono-
my, asking God for mercy and salvation using His own
Words.

(d) Request success in his audience before King Artaxerxes (1:11) - Nehemiah asked God to help him find favor
in the king's eyes.

(3) Please share your views of the differences and similarities
between Nehemiah's prayer (Nehemiah 1:5-11) and Ezra's
prayer (Ezra 9:6-15).

Suggested answer: The differences: Ezra prayed during
the evening sacrifice (Ezra 9:5), and it was a public prayer
in front of the Temple (Ezra 10:1). Nehemiah's prayer here
was not a public prayer, but a personal prayer before the
Lord during a time of fasting.

The similarities: Although the two prayers occurred at different time and places, both prayers were said with a broken and contrite spirit and both prayers openly acknowledged Israel's transgression. Ezra prayed "... because our
sins are higher than our heads and our guilt has reached to
the heavens. From the days of our ancestors until now, our
guilt has been great" (Ezra 9:6-7). Nehemiah said, "...I
confess the sins we Israelites, including myself and my
father's family, have committed against you. We have act-

ed very wickedly toward you ..." (Nehemiah 1:6-7). They both recognized Israel's current circumstances as subjugated captives resulting from disobeying God's teachings. Ezra prayed, "From the days of our ancestors until now, our guilt has been great. Because of our sins, we and our kings and our priests have been subjected to the sword and captivity, to pillage and humiliation at the hand of foreign kings, as it is today" (Ezra 9:7). Nehemiah also quoted Moses' words, "If you are unfaithful, I will scatter you among the nations" (Nehemiah 1:8).

Nonetheless, they both appealed to God for mercy, believing that God would acknowledge their repentance and once again bless His people. Ezra said, "Though we are slaves, our God has not forsaken us in our bondage..." (Ezra 9:9a) Nehemiah continued in Moses' words, "but if you return to me and obey my commands, then even if your exiled people are at the farthest horizon, I will gather them from there and bring them to the place I have chosen as a dwelling for my Name" (Nehemiah 1:9).

# Lesson 2: Inspecting the Walls Upon Being Called Back to Jerusalem

## ❖Fill in the blanks❖

(1) Then I said to the king, "If it pleases the king, and if your servant has found favor with you, I asked that you send me to (Judah), to the city of (my fathers' graves), so that I may rebuild it." (Nehemiah 2:5)

(2) "And the king granted me what I asked, for (the gracious hand of my God) was upon me." (Nehemiah 2:8)

(3) But when Sanbalat the Horonite and Tobiah (the Ammonite official), and Geshem the Arab heard of it, they mocked and ridiculed us, saying "What is this you are doing? Are you rebelling against the king?" (Nehemiah 2:19)

(4) The scripture in Nehemiah 2:15 says "...went up by way of the valley..." This valley refers to (Kidron Valley).

## ❖Scripture Study❖

1) How many months are there between the month of Chislev and the month of Nisan?

Suggested answer: From the month of Chislev to the month of Nisan, there are altogether four months in between. The month of Nisan is the New Year in Persia, which is also the first month in the Jewish calendar. It was in this month when God commanded Moses to tell the Israelites to prepare a lamb for each household for the first Passover. Following God's instruction, Moses led the Israelites on the Exodus journey after they ate the first Passover lamb. This is a very memorable month in the history of the Israelites. It was also in the month of Nisan when Nehemiah was granted his request to go back to Jerusalem.

2) In chapters 1 and 2 of the Book of Nehemiah, how many times did Nehemiah mention "the God of heaven?" What could be his intention for saying "the God of heaven" instead of "the Holy One of Israel"?

Suggested answer: Nehemiah used the term, "God of heaven", four times to call upon God. This might be his favorite term of calling God in his prayers, and it is the same term used by King Cyrus in his decree, which is recorded in Ezra 1:2. We can try to fathom the multiple meanings of calling God by this term.

- First, the scriptures in Genesis 1 clearly state that God is the Creator of the heavens and earth. When Nehemiah calls God "the God of heaven," he knows this God whom he worships is the God over all the creatures of the earth. By proclaiming "the God of heaven" instead of "the Holy One of Israel," theologically, Nehemiah acknowledges that God is not a familial or a tribal god.

When the Prophet Isaiah usd the term "The Holy One of Israel" in his prophecies, the emphasis was on the tie between God and His people. Often times, prophecies of God give hope and comfort to lift up the distressed people of God after warning them of their upcoming punishment as a consequence of their disobedience and refusal to turn from their wrong doings.

- Secondly, when Nehemiah prayed to "the God of heaven," he emphasizd the authority of God that is far beyond the limit of a tribe, but is over all nations, as what King Jehoshaphat announced in 2 Chronicles 20:6, "O Lord, God of our ancestors, are you not God in heaven? Do you not rule over all the kingdoms of the nations? In your hand are power and might, so that no one is able to withstand you." Though Nehemiah lived in the Susa palace under the reign of King Artaxerxes, he knew "the God of heaven" is the one who ultimately ruled over the Persian Empire of King Artaxerxes. Nehemiah's faith in God assurd him that every nation on earth, including the Persian Empire, is subject to his God who sits on the throne in heaven. Therefore, his God is "the God of heaven."

- Third, the covenant God had with Abraham, the Patriarch Father of the Israelites, is that "all the families of the earth shall be blessed" through Abraham. (Gen. 12:2-3) God's plan is to make the descendants of Abraham a priestly kingdom and a holy nation (Exodus 19:6), so that many nations on earth will be blessed by them. The Jews are taught to live according to this covenant. In Deuteronomy 4:39-40 Moses admonished the Israelites, "So acknowledge today and take to heart that the Lord is God in heaven above and on the earth beneath; there is no other. Keep his statutes and his commandments, which I am commanding you today for your own well-being and that of your descendants after you, so that you may long remain in the land that the Lord your God is giving you for all time." God's covenant with Abraham foreshadowed the covenant through the blood of Jesus Christ with all who are His children. As it is proclaimed in the Book of Revelation 15:3-4, "Great and amazing are your deeds, Lord God the Almighty! Just and true are your ways, King of the nations! Lord, who will not fear and glorify your name? For you alone are holy. All nations will come and worship before you, for your judgments have been revealed." By that day, every tribe, every nation and all the people on earth will worship Jesus Christ as their God. When Nehemiah prayed to "the God of heaven," he experienced God's gracious hands helping him as a result. His story assures us that "the God of heaven" listens to our prayers, watches over us, and rescues us from the evil one. He can surely guide us into the abundant life in Jesus Christ.

3) King Artaxerxes once made an order to prohibit the rebuilding of the walls of Jerusalem. Where in the Book of Ezra can we find this record?

Suggested answer: Ezra 4:6-22 tells us that after King Artaxerxes read the letter written by Governor Rehum, Shimashai the secretary, and their associates living in Samaria who used to slander the Jews, he gave the order to stop rebuilding Jerusalem, the city where the Jews used to worship God Jehovah.

## ❖Discussion and Sharing❖

(1). From Nehemiah's example of praying, waiting and take action, what principles can we learn and apply to our everyday lives?

Suggested answer: Prayer should always be the first thing that precedes anything and everything we do. Nehemiah is a very good spiritual leader. His way of doing things set a good example for today's Christians. His prayer in Chapter I was earnest and revealed his strong faith in God. He not only prayed, but also fasted, then waited patiently for God's own timing for His response to Nehemiah's prayers. Four months later, when the time of God has finally came, Nehemiah took the opportunity and told King Artaxerxes about his concerns. When the King asked what he wanted from him, again, he began by praying silently to make sure that the timing and his requests were from God. Nehemiah's sincerity in prayer, strong faith in God, and boldness to seize opportunity, makes him a great spiritual model for Christians.

There is a pattern that we can observe from Nehemiah's procedure of rebuilding Jerusalem. First, he prayed, then he waited upon God's guidance and revelation. He took on the God-given opportunity, carefully evaluated the situation, and followed through with thorough planning. Putting the project into implementation was the last step. It will be helpful to us to apply this pattern in our everyday lives.


(2) When Nehemiah obtained both the letter and the permission from the king, he gave all the credit to "the gracious hand of my God"! Have you ever experienced God's gracious hand upon you? Please share freely.

Suggested answer: the leader can list other incidents recorded in the Bible as encouragement to the students, when they share their experiences. In both Nehemiah 2:8 and 2:18, Nehemiah used the phrase "the gracious hand of God" to describe the mighty power of God and to convey the message that God successfully orchestrated all the events and happenings.

Ezra also frequently used a similar expression in Ezra 7:6,

7:9, 7:28, and 8:18. Both Nehemiah and Ezra were spiritual leaders of revival in the post-exilic period. They knew in their hearts that the rebuilding was not achieved by their own efforts, nor was it the result of the king's support and favor. Throughout the history of Israel, God's deliverance through His mighty hands are clearly recorded in the Bible for numerous events. such as in Exodus 6:1, 10:1, 14:4, and Isaiah 45:1-7. These scripture passages repeatedly tell us the truth about how this gracious God can move the heart of kings and leaders to achieve His plan for His people.

(3) How did Nehemiah request the Jewish people, the nobles, and the officials in Jerusalem for the rebuilding of the city wall?

Suggested answer: In Nehemiah 2:17-18, the attitude of Nehemiah, when he was calling the people to rebuild the walls, is an example for us today.

  (1) Nehemiah did not remain as an outsider and speak to the people in a superior tone as their authority, but humbly identified himself with the people there. He positioned himself as one of them ever since the beginning, by saying, "You see the trouble WE are in... Come, let us rebuild the wall of Jerusalem, so that WE may no longer suffer disgrace."

  (2) Objectively and practically he pointed out the severity

of the issues, by saying that Jerusalem "lies in ruins with its gates burned." His honesty and sincerity aroused the determination of the people to make a breakthrough after their long period of suffering and humiliation.

(3) He shared how he personally experienced the gracious hand of God upon him. His testimony encouraged and inspired the people in Jerusalem to have a strong faith in God.

# Lesson 3: Dividing the Work in Sections; Building the Walls Simultaneously in Unity

**Suggested answers for your reference:**

## ❖Fill in the blanks❖

(1) Then the high priest (Eliashib) set out to work with his fellow priests and rebuilt the Sheep Gate. They consecrated it and set up its doors; they consecrated it as far as the Tower of the Hundred and as far as the Tower of (Hananel). (Nehemiah 3:1)

(2) Nehemiah built on top of the stone wall which was built around 1200-1000 B.C. by the (Jebusites), to stabilize the eastern slopes of the city wall (using a stepped-stone structure), and to support their castles and palaces. In II Samuel,

I Kings and I & II Chronicles, It was called ("Millo"), meaning stabilizing the stone structure if the slope.

(3) In Nehemiah 3:8, there were goldsmiths and perfumemakers involved with the "restored Jerusalem as far as the (Broad Wall)." According to archaeological data, the "Broad Wall" was about 7 meters thick. The entire section of the "Broad Wall" was originally built by (King Hezekiah) of the Southern Kingdom (II Chronicles 32:5). Since this area was relatively flat, the city of Jerusalem could be defeated easily by enemies with battering rams, so they tried to make the walls thicker, and thus named it the "Broad Wall".

(4). In Nehemiah 3:16, the Nehemiah mentioned there was not the author of the Book of Nehemiah. He was the son of (Azbuk), ruler of the district of (Beth-zur), located in between Jerusalem and Hebron.

## ❖Scripture Study❖

(1) From the Bible, find the background of Eliashib, the high priest.

Suggested answer: Eliashib, the high priest, was the grandson of Jeshua, who served as the high priest when Zerubbabel led the people back to the Promised Land in the year 539 B.C.. Jeshua was a contemporary of Zerubbabel, whereas Eliashib was a contemporary of Nehemiah when Nehemiah came back to Jerusalem in the year 446 B.C..

The Book of Nehemiah cited Eliashib the high priest several times. He was appointed to oversee the chambers of the house of God, as recorded in Neh 13:4, 28; he had a close relationship with the enemies Sanballat and Tobiah. Later, he would become in-laws with Tobiah, and even prepared a large chamber in the Temple courtyard for Tobiah. As the high priest, Eliashib used his position for personal gain, despising the holy sanctuary, and disobeying God's commands about not intermarrying with gentiles. When Nehemiah returned from debriefing the king in the Susa Palace, he learned about these matters and was very angry (13:4-8).

(2) During the time of Nehemiah's rebuilding, there were ten gates at the Jerusalem City Walls. Find the names of the gates in Nehemiah 3.

Suggested answer: Jerusalem has gone through many changes throughout its history. The current Old City of Jerusalem has eight gates, which were built by Sultan Suleiman of the Ottoman Empire during the 16th century. There were ten gates in Jerusalem, however, during Nehemiah's era: the Sheep gate, the Fish Gate, the Old Gate, the Valley Gate, the Dung Gate, the Fountain Gate, the Water Gate, the Horse gate, the East Gate, and the Gate of Miphkad.

o The **Sheep Gate** was the gate for bringing sacrificial sheep to the entrance of the Temple; it was also called "the gate of Benjamin," and located in the northeastern corner of the city.

o The **Fish Gate** was located in the city's northwestern corner. During King Solomon's reign, the Fish Gate was a main gate. In II Chronicles 33:14, King Manasseh built an outer wall for the City of David, from the west side of Gihon in the valley, all the way to the Fish Gate. Serving as the main commercial port for fish trade, all kinds of fish from Tyre, Zidon, and the Sea of Galilee came through the Fish Gate of Jerusalem.

o The **Old Gate** during Nehemiah's time is possibly the Damascus Gate today, the most spectacular gate in Jerusalem today.

o The **Valley Gate** was one of the main gates on the west side of Jerusalem. It faced the Tyropoeon Valley.

o The **Dung Gate** was situated at the southernmost part of Jerusalem, at the junction of the Hinnom and Tyropoeon Valleys. Jeremiah 19:2 records, "and go out to the valley of the son of Hinnom at the entry of the Potsherd Gate, and proclaim there the words that I tell you." God also moved the prophet Jeremiah to declare God's Word there.

o The **Fountain Gate** was located near the Pool of Siloah – or the "Pool of Siloam." This site was mentioned along with King Hezekiah, as recorded in II Kings 20 and II Chronicles 32.

o The **Water Gate** was located by the Gihon Spring, next to the Kidron Valley. During early 7th century B.C., when the Assyrian attacked Jerusalem, in order to prepare for the long war, King Hezekiah of Judah ordered his people to dig a waterway, connecting the "Gihon Springs" outside the city wall to the inner city "Pool of Siloam." The waterway was more than 500 meters long, and 5-10 meters deep. Even today, there is spring water flowing through this waterway.

o The **Horse Gate** served as the east gate of Jerusalem, and as a pathway leading to the palace door from the Temple. In Jeremiah 31:40, the following record of Jerusalem was given: "... all the fields as far as the brook (Wadi) Kidron, to the corner of the Horse Gate toward the east, shall be sacred to the Lord."

o The historical **East Gate** is likely today's Golden Gate, facing the Mount of Olives. However, it has been sealed by the Muslims for several centuries.

o The **Gate of Miphkad** is also referred to as the "Review Gate," and located at the northern end of the east wall. Very likely, it is also the "Gate of the Guard" mentioned in Nehemiah 12:39.

(3) Among the people rebuilding the walls, Nehemiah assigned each group of people to be responsible for constructing one segment. Occasionally, however a few of

them were put in charge of building more than one segment. Who were they?

Suggested answer:

1) Meremoth was the son of Uriah and grandson of Hakkoz. (3:4,21) When Ezra went back to Jerusalem, he took all the gold, silver and precious vessels offered by people to the Temple, weighed them and turned them over to the priest Meremoth. It was obvious that Meremoth was an honest and faithful man. Here we also learn that after he finished repairing his first assigned section, he continued to repair another section (3:21).

2) The Tekoites were mentioned in Nehemiah 3:5, 27. Tekoa was located in the province of Judah, south of Bethlehem, about seventeen kilometers from Jerusalem. It was an agricultural town and home of the prophet Amos. Although the Tekoa nobles did not want to participate in the construction of walls due to concerns of political risk, nevertheless, the Tekoites were willing to work more than the others. They really valued their relationship with God, and didn't allow their faith to be affected by worldly concerns.

3) Hanun (3:13, 30) – He started from the Valley Gate and continued building about a thousand cubits (about 1,500 feet) of the wall; this was not a small job. Later, he also built another section between the East Gate and Meshullam's house.

4) Meshullam, son of Berechiah (3:4, 6, 30) – Meshullam served as priest in the Temple. After he built some walls against his house, he continued repairing the wall between the Fish Gate and Old Gate, working together with Joiada. However, his daughter married Johanan, the son of Tobiah. After the marriage, Meshullam often mentioned his in-law's good deeds to Nehemiah.

## ❖Discussion and Sharing❖

(1) Nehemiah repaired the walls starting from the Sheep Gate and the Tower of Hananel. Based on Jeremiah 31:38-40 and John 10:7-9, what is the significance of the Sheep Gate and the Tower of Hananel?

Suggested answer: Jeremiah 31:38-40 says, "The days are surely coming, says the Lord, when the city shall be rebuilt for the Lord from the tower of Hananel to the Corner Gate. And the measuring line shall go out farther, straight to the hill Gareb, and shall then turn to Goah. The whole valley of the dead bodies and the ashes, and all the fields as far as the brook Kidron, to the corner of the Horse Gate toward the east, shall be sacred to the Lord. It shall never again be uprooted or overthrown." Jesus also said in John 10:7, 9: "'I am the gate for the sheep ... I am the gate. Whoever enters by me will be saved, and will come in and go out and find pasture.'"

When the Israelites offered sacrifice, they brought the unblemished sheep through the Sheep Gate to the Temple entrance. Passing through the Sheep Gate was a symbol of man's repentance, bringing a sacrifice to God, praying for His pardon, and asking for forgiveness. The rebuilding of the tower of Hananel confirmed the prophecy by Jeremiah. As for the Israelites, reconstruction of the tower of Hananel, along with the walls, meant God's anger was turned away, and that He would restore Israel. This was the realization of God's grace to forgive, and demonstration of His people's desire to sanctify themselves and the holy city of Jerusalem, and to restore their covenant relationship with God.

(2). Nehemiah recorded detailed information about each person who participated in repairing the walls. Is any of them inspiring to you?

Suggested answer: The people who rebuilt the walls during the time of Nehemiah shared the same goal, namely, the building up of the community and the restoration of relationship with God through their dedication and holiness. As their names are listed in Nehemiah, we believe that God has recorded their names in heaven along with others who build up His Church—the body of Christ. For Christians today, through the Book of Revelation, we have a greater revelation than the people did in the time of Nehemiah. Jesus Christ said, "If you conquer, I will make you a pillar in the temple of my God; you will never go out of it. I will write on you the name of my God, and the name of the city of my God, the new Jerusalem that comes down from my God out of heaven." (Rev. 3:12)

(3). The people who built and reconstructed the walls of Jerusalem came from different hometowns and walks of life, including the young and old, male and female. As a Christian, how do you feel about this kind of collaboration?

Suggested answer: The list of people who rebuilt the wall reminds us of the earlier stories of Israel's "mighty warriors" (2 Sam 23:8) and their deeds of valor against Israel's enemies. However, the heroes here include priests, goldsmiths, perfume makers, district rulers, temple servants, gate keepers, and merchants. They are ordinary people chosen by God, seeking to please Him by using their skills and resources, and possibly endangering their lives to dwell with God in Jerusalem.

The main reason that the work of repairing and rebuilding the city walls was able to proceed was because everybody participated, from rulers, to priests, to temple personnel to merchants, to people with their families. Even villagers who lived in the distant rural areas of the Judah province joined in to reconstruct the walls. As they built the walls, they also built up and demonstrated their community spirit.

This is a perfect picture of unity, not just in connection to the Israelites in the Old Testament, but also depicting the unity of Christians in Jesus Christ today. As Paul wrote in I Corinthians 12, "Now there are varieties of gifts, but the same Spirit; and there are varieties of service, but the same Lord; and there are varieties of activities, but it is the same God who activates all of them in everyone. (12:4~6) ... For just as the body is one and has many members, and all the members of the body, though many, are one body, so it is with Christ. For in the one Spirit we were all baptized into one body—Jews or Greeks, slaves or free—and we were all made to drink of one Spirit. Indeed, the body does not consist of one member but of many. (12:12~14)... Now you are the body of Christ and individually members of it." (12:27)

---

## Lesson 4: Fearing not the Enemies with Strong Faith
## Rectifying Internal Conflicts and Helping the Poor

---

**Suggested answers for your reference:**

### ❖Fill in the blanks❖

(1) But when (Sanballat) and (Tobiah) and the (Arabs) and the

(Ammonites) and the (Ashdodites) heard that the repairing of the walls of Jerusalem was going forward and the gaps were beginning to be closed, they were very angry. (Nehemiah 4:7)

(2) The burden bearers carried their loads in such a way that each (labored on the work) with one hand and with the other held a (weapon). And each of the builders had his (sword) strapped at his side while he built. The man who (sounded the trumpet) was beside me. (Nehemiah 4:17-18)

(3) Moreover from the time that I was appointed to be their governor in the (land of Judah), from the twentieth year to the (thirty-second) year of King Artaxerxes, twelve years, neither I nor my brothers ate the food allowance of the governor. The former governors who were before me laid heavy burdens on the people, and took food and wine from them, besides (forty shekels) of silver. Even their servants lorded it over the people. But I did not do so, because of the (fear of God). (Nehemiah 5:14-15)

(4). So the wall was finished on the (twenty-fifth) day of the month Elul, in (fifty-two) days. (Nehemiah 6:15)

## ❖Scripture Study❖

(1) Besides the famine that happened when Nehemiah served as the governor in the land of Judah, are you aware of any other famines in the land of Canaan that were recorded in the Bible?

Suggested answer: From the records in the Bible, we learn that famine did not only take place during the times of Nehemiah, but also in the times of Abraham (Gen 12:10), Isaac (Gen 26:1), Joseph (Gen 41:27, 54), Ruth (Ruth 1:1), King David (2 Sa 21:1), Elijah (1 Ki 18:2), Elisha (2 Ki 4:38), and Claudius (Acts 11:28).

Biblical scripture reminds us of God's disciplinary actions against His children when they are rebellious. God has made His decrees known to His children since the days of Moses (see Deu 28). However, God's people failed to faithfully follow God's words. They did not listen to God's words taught by His prophets. Prophet Amos announced the words of God, saying, "Thus says the Lord: For three transgressions of Israel, and for four, I will not revoke the punishment; because they sell the righteous for silver, and the needy for a pair of sandals— they who trample the head of the poor into the dust of the earth, and push the afflicted out of the way; father and son go into the same girl, so that my holy name is profaned; they lay themselves down beside every altar on garments taken in pledge; and in the house of their God they drink wine bought with fines they imposed." (Amos 2:6-8)

In Jeremiah 14:17-18, the prophet describes how heartbroken God was when he had to discipline His children by saying, "Let my eyes run down with tears night and day, and let them not cease, for the virgin daughter—my people—is struck down with a crushing blow, with a very grievous wound. If I go out into the field, look—those killed by the sword! And if I enter the city, look—those sick with famine! For both prophet and priest ply their trade throughout the land, and have no knowledge."

(2)  In Nehemiah 4:20, Nehemiah proclaims, "Our God will fight for us." Please locate other similar incidents in the Bible where God fights for His people.

Suggested answer: The Bible is one coherent story about God's warfare against evil. God is holy, and he raises holy wars against evil throughout the ages. When God delivered the Jews out of Egypt, God destroyed the Egyptian army and buried them in the Red Sea. When Joshua led the Israelites into the Promised Land, God fought for them and gave them the land of Canaan just as He promised Abraham. When the kings of Israel ruled over the kingdom according to the will of God, God subdued their enemies before them. Battles of such kind can be found in the following scriptures: Deu 3:22-29, 20:1-4; Jos 6:1-16, Jos 10:5-15, Jos 10:40-42, Judges 4:14-21, 2 Sam 5:22-24, 2 Chr. 32:7-8. They are all good illustrations of how God fights on behalf of the Jews to eliminate their enemies of flesh and blood.

As the history of the Israelites continued, we witness how God fought against Israel and Judah when they were ruled by kings who did evil in the eyes of the Lord and thus brought both the northern and southern kingdoms to an end. When the people of God were exiled into the hands of foreign empires, the merciful God fought once again for them and saved them from their oppressors. Gaining confidence from all these historical records, Nehemiah trusted that his righteous God, who listened to prayers of His people, would definitely disrupt the plots of the enemies and fight for the Israelites.

(3) Please summarize the Mosaic laws from Exodus 20:1-11 and Leviticus 25:39-43 concerning the proper treatment of the farm workers and domestic helpers who work for their fellow Jews.

Suggested answer: In Mosaic Law, God does not prohibit Israelites from hiring domestic helpers or buying slaves to work for them. However, there are clear restrictions that the Israelites should not enslave other Jews, but treat them as workers or domestic helpers. In the year of Sabbath, which is the seventh year, the workers must be offered the freedom to leave the household with their own wives and families. A female slave, if later married to the family, must be provided with food, clothing and shelter for the rest of her life. The reason for such regulations is that God views every Israelite as His own property. In Leviticus 25:55, God says, "For to me the people of Israel are servants; they are my servants whom I brought out from the land of Egypt: I am the Lord your God." Therefore, no Israelite is allowed to enslave other fellow Israelites. The Israelites are allowed only to take gentile slaves as their possession and pass them onto their children.

Apparently, in the time of Nehemiah, the Jews did not follow what was required by the law of Moses when dealing with their fellow Israelites. Nehemiah knew that this was one of the main reasons why the Israelites suffered the pain and humiliation of subjugation. Nehemiah was distressed to see how greed drove the Israelites to their old ways of mistreating their fellow Israelites, regardless of God's words. Although they had returned to their homeland, the Jews repeatedly disobeyed God and valued short-term financial gain and personal interest more than trusting God's promise, that they would enjoy a spiritually and materially abundant life in the Promised Land when they followed the ordinances of the Lord.

## ❖Discussion and Sharing❖

(1). How should we interpret Nehemiah's prayer in Nehemiah 4:4-5?

Suggested answer: In Nehemiah 4:4-5 Nehemiah prayed, "Hear, O our God, for we are despised; turn their taunt back on their own heads, and give them over as plunder in a land of captivity. Do not cover their guilt, and do not let their sin be blotted out from your sight; for they have hurled insults in the face of the builders." First we should know that this prayer is not a vengeful curse. Nehemiah is appealing to God to rise up and block the evil plots of the enemies. This is in accordance with God's righteousness. Secondly, this prayer demonstrates Nehemiah's zealous passion for the glory of the name of God and the divine ministry that God has called him to. Therefore, he prayed and asked God not to allow God's people to be despised and hence bring humiliation to God's name. As God announces in Jeremiah 17:10 that, "I the Lord test the mind and search the heart, to give to all according to their ways, according to the fruit of their doings."

After all, when Nehemiah prayed that God would not cover the sins of the enemies, he was praying that God would protect His people. Nehemiah knew the love and kindness of God. What he prayed was is to vindicate the unjust suffering of the Israelites, which is not in conflict with Jesus' teaching to forgive one's enemies.

(2) Are there any areas damaged by enemies in your spiritual life, like the broken city walls of Jerusalem? Have you ever heard God's "trumpet call" alerting you to be on guard against the enemies?

Suggested answer: Everything that has happened in our life since childhood has a huge impact on our emotions, the way we think, our personal character, and our value systems. Are we gloomy, critical, and unforgiving? Are we proud, greedy, or in the habit of lying? Often times, what we are accustomed to are the trends of the world, which are at odds with biblical principles. Whenever we sense that certain behaviors or thoughts of ours are against God's teaching, we should be alarmed, as those wall builders who heard the sound of the trumpet. The sound of the trumpet, sounded out by the Holy Spirit, is a warning that we are in a battle with our spiritual enemies.

We can either choose to remain the same and pretend not to hear it or to earnestly seek God's guidance in our spiritual battle against the enemy. How we respond to the trumpet call is our choice. If we are obedient to God's calling, God will help us due to His faithfulness. From question #2 in Scripture Studies, we have learned how God fights for His people. Likewise, God will send His mighty messengers and gather the spiritual resources to help us fight against our spiritual enemies, who attack the broken areas of our lives. We are taught by Scripture in Ephesians chapter 6 that, "Finally, be strong in the Lord and in the strength of his power. Put on the whole armor of God, so that you may be able to stand against the wiles of the devil. For our struggle is not against enemies of blood and flesh, but against the rulers, against the authorities, against the cosmic powers of this present darkness, against the spiritual forces of evil in the heavenly places. Therefore, take up the whole armor of God, so that you may be able to withstand on that evil day, and having done everything, to stand firm." (Eph. 6:10-13)

(3) In Philippians 2:3-5 Paul says, "Do nothing from selfish ambition or conceit, but in humility regard others as better than yourselves. Let each of you look not to your own interests, but to the interests of others. Let the same mind be in you that was in Christ Jesus." This was exactly what Nehemiah did when he was governor in Jerusalem, leading the people to rebuild the walls. Are your deeds evidence of what you claim to believe in Scripture?

Suggested answer: Encourage students to share their own experiences.

During the discussion, the teacher can share with students that our salvation is not earned by our good deeds. We are not justified by our deeds, as what the book of Romans proclaims, "Therefore, since we are justified by faith, we have peace with God through our Lord Jesus Christ, through whom we have obtained access to this grace in which we stand; and we boast in our hope of sharing the glory of God." (Romans 5:1-2) However, Scripture also reminds us that, "So faith by itself, if it has no works, is dead." (James 2:17) Paul also continues in Romans 5:3-5, "And not only that, but we also boast in our sufferings, knowing that suffering produces endurance, and endurance produces character, and character produces hope, and hope does not disappoint us, because God's love has been poured into our hearts through the Holy Spirit that has been given to us."

The Scriptures are the words of God. They are not merely a reference for us to decide whether we should follow them or not. They guide us to conduct our lives in a way that pleases God, so that we can receive the abundant life promised by Jesus Christ. "Scripture teaches us how to follow Jesus and take up our cross daily because Christians have tasted the love of God. We can now worship our Lord by obeying Him be His ambassadors in this world." God is faithful and His words are all true. Nehemiah trusted God and did not waver in the midst of all the suffering and challenges that he encountered / that came again blm. His way of life is a witness of the truth of Scriptures. We know that in all circumstances we are called to honor God and follow His words.

# Lesson 5: Casting Lots to Settle and Guard the Holy City

**Suggested answers for your reference:**

## ❖Fill in the blanks❖

(1) I said to them, "The gates of Jerusalem are not to be opened until the (sun is hot); while the (gate-keepers) are still standing guard, let them shut and bar the doors." (Nehemiah 7:3)

(2) Now the leaders of the people lived in Jerusalem; and the rest of the people cast lots to bring (one) out of ten to live in the holy city Jerusalem, while (nine-tenths) remained in the other towns. (Nehemiah 11:1)

(3) These were in the days of Joiakim son of Jeshua son of Jozadak, and in the days of the governor (Nehemiah) and of the priest (Ezra), the scribe. (Nehemiah 12:26)

(4) From the list provided in Nehemiah 11:4-9, we learned that the people of (Judah and Benjamin) lived in the city of Jerusalem, other than the priests and those who worked in the temple at that time.

## ❖Scripture Study❖

(1) What is the daric?

Suggested answer: The daric, named after King Darius,

was a golden coin used within the Persian Empire. It bore the image of King Darius armed with a bow and arrow. One daric weighed about 8.5 grams. The Book of Ezra recordes that when the Israelites returned to Jerusalem, "According to their resources they gave to the building fund sixty-one thousand darics of gold, five thousand minas of silver, and one hundred priestly robes." (Ezra 2:69) 61,000 darics of gold weighed about 500 kilograms. For more details, please refer to the description of "Daric" in "Relic Monthly" Aug. 2014 on https://sowim.org/2014/08/01/august-2014-2/

(2). Why was the number of the Levites far smaller than the number of the priests on Nehemiah's list?

Suggested answer: When Zerubbabel led the Israelites back from captivity, there were only seventy-four Levites as recorded in Ezra 2:40. When Ezra returned to Jerusalem upon King Cyrus' edict, he specifically summoned around forty Levites to come with him after he found that there were not any Levites among the returnees (Ezra 8:18-19). Nehemiah 11:18 recorded "the Levites in the holy city were two hundred eighty-four", while there were 1,192 priests. Similarly, as recorded in Ezra 2:40, the Levites were far fewer than the priests among the returnees.

When the Israelites were led out of Egypt, "the Lord spoke to Moses, saying: I hereby accept the Levites from among the Israelites as substitutes for all the firstborn that open the womb among the Israelites. The Levites shall be mine." (Numbers 3:11-12) At the Lord's command, therefore, Joshua did not allot land to the Levites when he led the Israelites into the land of Canaan.

The Bible also says, "These are the inheritances that the Israelites received in the land of Canaan, which the priest Eleazar, and Joshua son of Nun, and the heads of the families of the tribes of the Israelites distributed to them. Their inheritance was by lot, as the Lord had commanded Moses for the nine and one-half tribes. For Moses had given an inheritance to the two and one-half tribes beyond the Jordan; but to the Levites he gave no inheritance among them...but only towns to live in, with their pasture lands for their flocks and herds." (Joshua 14:1-4)

After the subjugation of Judah and the destroying of the Temple, some Levites took on other professions and became unfamiliar with the work in the Temple. Furthermore, with no land in Israel, the Levite's willingness to return was not high. Therefore, we found far fewer Levites than priests in the genealogical record of the returnees.

(3) Are there other incidents in the Bible where people made decisions by casting lots?

Suggested answer: We can see the use of casting lots recorded in several places in the Bible, such as: Numbers

26:55-56; 1 Chronicles 24:5, 25:8, and Luke 1:9. However, God can use different methods of making his will known to us.

In John 14:16-17 Jesus says, "And I will ask the Father, and he will give you another Advocate, to be with you forever. This is the Spirit of truth, whom the world cannot receive, because it neither sees him nor knows him. You know him, because he abides with you, and he will be in you." Jesus further assures us that: "But the Advocate, the Holy Spirit, whom the Father will send in my name, will teach you everything, and remind you of all that I have said to you." (John 14:26) Being a Christian living in the New Testament era, we don't have to depend on casting lots to make decisions. We can expect that God will reveal His heart to us through His Word in the scriptures, our inner conviction by the Holy Spirit, and the verification of His guidance from our circumstances. God is a sovereign God, hence we can fully trust Him for His guidance.

## ❖Discussion and Sharing❖

(1). If, like Nehemiah you run short on people and resources when starting a business or working on a project, like rebuilding Jerusalem, what would your attitude be and what would you do?

Suggested answer: When we focus on work or hope to succeed in a business venture, in order to save cost in a shortage of funds, we may work overtime, borrow money from friends and family, or even deed out our properties. Such hard-working attitudes and financial planning are completely different from how Nehemiah managed the rebuilding of Jerusalem. He put Hanani and Hananiah in charge of Jerusalem. While personnel were few, he deployed temple gatekeepers, the singers, as well as the Levites, to stand as guards at the gates.

Nehemiah's rebuilding plan was not to prove his own caliber or to acquire wealth; his plan was formulated with a mission to fulfill prophecy, which is to restore Jerusalem's former glory and historical sacred standing. He made a comprehensive plan under the plight of personnel and resource shortages. He valued the safety of people in Jerusalem, and he approached his plan with a God-fearing attitude and a desire to fulfill God's will.

Likewise, before we embark on a project or entrepreneurship, we need to examine whether our motives please God, and should adjust the pace of executing the plan accordingly if needed. When we encounter a bottleneck such as resource and personnel shortage, we must be honest with God and ourselves, learning from Nehemiah who was a "faithful man and feared God." (Neh 7:2) We must concentrate on praying to God, reading the Bible regularly, and seeking wisdom and strategies from God because His word is "a lamp to my feet, and a light to my path." (Psalms

119:105) If there are mature men and women of God around, their advice can be very valuable as well.

(2) Why did Nehemiah want the returnees to move into Jerusalem?

Suggested answer: Nehemiah clearly knew that even though the construction of the wall was completed, in order to defend Jerusalem from the enemy's attack, there must be people living in the city to watch over one another. When they guarded the section of the city wall right in front of their houses and helped one another to strengthen Jerusalem's self-defense capacity, the city was kept safe from enemy attack.

From the perspective of historical heritage, the Bible tells us, "David was thirty years old when he began to reign, and he reigned for forty years. At Hebron, he reigned over Judah for seven years and six months; at Jerusalem, he reigned over all Israel and Judah for thirty-three years." (2 Samuel 5:4-5) Since the time when David became king, Jerusalem had been the capital city of Judah until 586 B.C. when Babylonian King Nebuchadnezzar captured Judah by force. Later, the Persian King Cyrus gave an edict to allow the Israelites to return to their native land to rebuild the Temple. King Darius then permitted the rebuilding work to resume. After that, King Artaxerxes appointed Ezra the scribe to restore the temple system and appointed

Nehemiah as the governor to rebuild Jerusalem. To be able to rebuild Jerusalem after approximately 150 years of desolation was not just an opportunity for the Jews to resume their glorious past, but also to fulfill the mission of continuing their ethnic cultural heritage.

From the perspective of faith, the prophet Zechariah prophesied, "Thus says the Lord of hosts: I am jealous for Zion with great jealousy, and I am jealous for her with great wrath. Thus says the Lord: I will return to Zion, and will dwell in the midst of Jerusalem; Jerusalem shall be called the faithful city, and the mountain of the Lord of hosts shall be called the holy mountain. Thus says the Lord of hosts: Old men and old women shall again sit in the streets of Jerusalem, each with staff in hand because of their great age. And the streets of the city shall be full of boys and girls playing in its streets. Thus says the Lord of hosts: Even though it seems impossible to the remnant of this people in these days, should it also seem impossible to me, says the Lord of hosts?" (Zechariah 8:2-6) Nehemiah brought leaders, heads of families, and people back to Jerusalem so that the city was populated and became prosperous. Thus, God's prophecies through the prophet were fulfilled.

(3) Based on your study of the book of Nehemiah so far, please list three similarities and three differences between you

and Nehemiah. Based on what you have studied so far, what are Nehemiah's strengths that are worth learning from?

Suggested answer: Let each student share freely the similarities and differences between themselves and Nehemiah.

Nehemiah has many strengths which are worth learning from:

1) Nehemiah is a man who studies God's words.
   - He firmly believes that the Law of Moses is the source of God's blessings, disciplines and promises to the Israelites.

2) Nehemiah is a man who prays.
   - He confesses and repents before God. (Neh 1:6-7)
   - He seeks God's will patiently. (Neh 1:11)
   - He is intimate with God. (Neh 1:5, 2:8b, 5:19)
   - He has a habit of praying to God anytime and anywhere. (Neh 2:4; 4:9)

3) Nehemiah is a man who fears God.
   - He sympathizes with the burden of the people and does not take the salary of a governor. (Neh 5:14-15)
   - He denounces acts of financial greed when lending money and leads by example. (Neh 5:9-10)

4) Nehemiah is a man who devises thorough plans.
   - He presents detailed needs of material and staff deployment when King Artaxerxes grants his return to

the province of Judah. (Neh 2:6-9)

- He divides the entire construction project into 45 sections and builds each of them simultaneously. (Neh 3:1-32)
- After the construction of the wall, Nehemiah resettles the Israelites to live in Jerusalem. (Neh 11:1-2)

5) Nehemiah is a man who does not fear or flinch, but who is full of faith in God.

- He replies to the enemies, "The God of heaven is the one who will give us success." (Neh 2:20)
- When confronted with repeated ridicule, intimidation, and threats from enemies, he shows no fear. (Neh 4:9, 20; 6:1-14)

# Lesson 6: Reading of the Law, Signing the Covenant
# Dedication of the City Walls, Managing Services in the Temple

**Suggested answers for your reference:**

## ❖Fill in the blanks❖

(1) All the people gathered together into (the square before the Water Gate). They told the scribe (Ezra) to bring the book of the Law of Moses, which the Lord had given to Israel.

(Neh 8:1)

(2) And day by day, from the first day to the last day, (Ezra) read from the book of the law of God. They kept the festival (seven days); and on the eighth day there was a solemn assembly, according to the ordinance. (Neh 8:18)

(3) You are the Lord, the God who chose (Abram) and brought him out of Ur of the Chaldeans and gave him the name (Abraham); and you found his heart faithful before you, and made with him a covenant to give to his descendants the land of the (Canaanite), the Hittite, the Amorite, the Perizzite, the (Jebusite), and the Girgashite; and you have fulfilled your promise, for you are righteous. (Neh 9:7-8)

(4) For in the days of (David and Asaph) long ago there was a leader of the singers, and there were songs of praise and thanksgiving to God. In the days of Zerubbabel and in the days of (Nehemiah) all Israel gave the daily portions for the singers and the gatekeepers. They set apart that which was for the (Levites); and the Levites set apart that which was for the (descendants of Aaron). (Neh 12:46-47)

## ❖Scripture Study❖

(1) Based on Leviticus 23:24-44, list the Jewish festivals that occur in the seventh month of the Jewish religious calender.

Suggested answer: The new year of the Jewish religious calender starts in the seventh month (Month of Tishri), which is between September and October on the Gregorian Calendar. It is an important month for the Jews. The first day of the seventh month is "Rosh Hashanah", also the Jewish New Year. According to Leviticus 23:24-25, the Lord asked Moses to "speak to the people of Israel, saying: In the seventh month, on the first day of the month, you shall observe a day of complete rest, a holy convocation commemorated with trumpet blasts. You shall not work at your occupations; and you shall present the Lord's offering by fire."

The tenth day of this month is "Yom Kippur", the Day of Atonement. The passages of Leviticus 23:27-30 say, "Now, the tenth day of this seventh month is the day of atonement; it shall be a holy convocation for you: you shall deny yourselves and present the Lord's offering by fire; and you shall do no work during that entire day; for it is a day of atonement, to make atonement on your behalf before the Lord your God. For anyone who does not practice self-denial during that entire day shall be cut off from the people. And anyone who does any work during that entire day, such a one I will destroy from the midst of the people."

The fifteenth day is the "Festival of Booths", during which time the Israelites lived in booths made of branches in remembrance of God's provision and protection during the exodus from Egypt. For forty years, they had daily provision of manna, their clothes did not wear out, and their feet did not swell. The Festival of Booths lasted for seven days. Scripture passages detailing this festival can be found in Leviticus 23:34-43, as well as in Numbers 29:12-34 and Deuteronomy 31:11-13.

There is a Solemn Assembly on the eighth day. According to Leviticus 23:36, 39, "on the eighth day you shall observe a holy convocation and present the Lord's offerings by fire; it is a solemn assembly; you shall not work at your occupations…Now, the fifteenth day of the seventh month, when you have gathered in the produce of the land, you shall keep the festival of the Lord, lasting seven days; a complete rest on the first day, and a complete rest on the eighth day."

(2) God instructed the Israelites to observe both the Sabbath Day and the Sabbatical Year in the Law of Moses. What is the Sabbatical Year? Please refer to Scripture recorded in Exodus 23:10-11, Deuteronomy 15:1-3 and Leviticus 25:3-7.

Suggested answer: God instructed the Israelites to observe both the Sabbath Day and the Sabbatical Year in the Laws of Moses. What is the Sabbatical Year? Please refer to Scripture recorded in Exodus 23:10-11, Deuteronomy 15:1-3 and Leviticus 25:3-7.

Exodus 23:10-11: "For six years you shall sow your land

and gather in its yield; but the seventh year you shall let it rest and lie fallow, so that the poor of your people may eat; and what they leave the wild animals may eat. You shall do the same with your vineyard, and with your olive orchard." Deuteronomy 15:1-3: "Every seventh year you shall grant a remission of debts. And this is the manner of the remission: every creditor shall remit the claim that is held against a neighbor, not exacting it of a neighbor who is a member of the community, because the Lord's remission has been proclaimed. Of a foreigner you may exact it, but you must remit your claim on whatever any member of your community owes you."

Leviticus 25:3-7: "Six years you shall sow your field, and six years you shall prune your vineyard, and gather in their yield; but in the seventh year there shall be a sabbath of complete rest for the land, a sabbath for the Lord: you shall not sow your field or prune your vineyard. You shall not reap the aftergrowth of your harvest or gather the grapes of your unpruned vine: it shall be a year of complete rest for the land. You may eat what the land yields during its sabbath—you, your male and female slaves, your hired and your bound laborers who live with you; for your livestock also, and for the wild animals in your land and all its yield shall be for food."

(3) Which books of the Bible recorded the Israelites' exodus

from Egypt?

Suggested answer: The Book of Exodus recorded how God called Moses to lead the Israelites out of Egypt, how He inflicted the ten plagues on Egypt, how He led the Israelites across the Red Sea on dry land, as well as the events during the Israelites' forty years in the wilderness. The prayer in Nehemiah 9:9-21 is an epitome of the Book of Exodus. According to 1 Kings 6:1, "In the four hundred eightieth year after the Israelites came out of the land of Egypt, in the fourth year of Solomon's reign over Israel"— We can estimate that the Israelites came out of the land of Egypt in 1446 B.C., which was 480 years prior to the fourth year of Solomon's reign over Israel (966 B.C.). Although scholars differ in their views on the exact year of the exodus, Israel's exodus from Egypt and entry into the land of Canaan are actual historical events supported by archeological evidence.

## ❖Discussion and Sharing❖

(1) What does tithing mean to Christians?

Suggested answer: Tithing first appeared when Abraham (originally Abram), after rescuing his nephew Lot, met Melchizedek king of Salem who welcomed Abram with bread and wine. In Genesis 14:18-20, it was recorded, "He blessed him and said, 'Blessed be Abram by God Most High, maker of heaven and earth; and blessed be God Most

High, who has delivered your enemies into your hand!'
And Abram gave him one-tenth of everything." Melchizedek, introduced in the Bible as "Priest of the Most High God", blessed Abram, and Abram gave him one-tenth of his possessions.

Nehemiah 10:37 recorded that the people brought the wine and the oil and the tithes from their land to the Levites in the House of God. This was in accordance with the statutes and ordinances that God commanded the Israelites through his servant Moses. As it is written in Numbers 18:20-21, "Then the Lord said to Aaron: You shall have no allotment in their land, nor shall you have any share among them; I am your share and your possession among the Israelites. To the Levites I have given every tithe in Israel for a possession in return for the service that they perform, the service in the tent of meeting." Also in Leviticus 27:30, "All tithes from the land, whether the seed from the ground or the fruit from the tree, are the Lord's; they are holy to the Lord." Therefore, Christians tithe is based on the commandment that one tenth of the produce from the ground, which is our income, is holy to the Lord.

Yet, despite the earnestness of the speaker, the listeners continued in their own way. Tithing was hard for the Jews to keep consistently, so God sent the prophet Malachi to instruct them, "For I the Lord do not change; therefore you, O children of Jacob, have not perished. Ever since the days of your ancestors you have turned aside from my statutes and have not kept them. Return to me, and I will return to you, says the Lord of hosts. But you say, 'How shall we return? Will anyone rob God?' Yet you are robbing me! But you say, 'How are we robbing you?' In your tithes and offerings! You are cursed with a curse, for you are robbing me—the whole nation of you!" (Malachi 3:6-9). However, God's loving will is to bless His children, as long as they repent. Therefore God continues to say, "Bring the full tithe into the storehouse, so that there may be food in my house, and thus put me to the test, says the Lord of hosts; see if I will not open the windows of heaven for you and pour down for you an overflowing blessing. I will rebuke the locust for you, so that it will not destroy the produce of your soil; and your vine in the field shall not be barren, says the Lord of hosts. Then all nations will count you happy, for you will be a land of delight, says the Lord of hosts." (Malachi 3:10-12)

When Jesus came, he found that even though the Pharisees tithed, their inner motives were not right. So he condemned them: "Woe to you, scribes and Pharisees, hypocrites! For you tithe mint, dill, and cummin, and have neglected the weightier matters of the law: justice and mercy and faith. It is these you ought to have practiced without neglecting the others. You blind guides! You strain out a gnat but swallow a camel!" (Matthew 23:23-24)

For Christians today, we not only need to obey the teaching on tithing, but also need to understand that tithing cannot be used to cover up our impure motives. God judges our hearts. Tithing must stem from a heart of genuine love for God and people. It should neither be used for earning the label of a "good Christian" nor for showing off our good behavior. If we could selflessly give to our own earthly children, how much more could we give to our beloved God who richly blesses his children? Let us tithe with joyful and thankful hearts, while also observing Jesus' weightier commands regarding justice, mercy, and faith. As Apostle Paul exhorts in Romans 12:1-2, "I appeal to you therefore, brothers and sisters, by the mercies of God, to present your bodies as a living sacrifice, holy and acceptable to God, which is your spiritual worship. Do not be conformed to this world, but be transformed by the renewing of your minds, so that you may discern what is the will of God—what is good and acceptable and perfect."

(2) How do you address God in your prayers? Why?
Suggested answer: Students should be encouraged to share freely. Our favorite ways of addressing God provide a glimpse of how each of us personally and spiritually relate to God. Listening to everyone's perspectives can help us more richly understand multiple aspects of God

(3) Why do Christians today no longer need to obey the laws on sacrifices according to the Law of Moses?

Suggested answer: As Nehemiah said when he, together with Ezra, the priests and the Levites, led the Israelites in a repentant prayer, "our ancestors acted presumptuously and stiffened their necks and did not obey your commandments" (Neh 9:16); and, "But after they had rest, they again did evil before you, and you abandoned them to the hands of their enemies, so that they had dominion over them; yet when they turned and cried to you, you heard from heaven, and many times you rescued them according to your mercies. And you warned them in order to turn them back to your law. Yet they acted presumptuously and did not obey your commandments, but sinned against your ordinances, by the observance of which a person shall live. They turned a stubborn shoulder and stiffened their neck and would not obey." (Neh 9:28~29) Whenever our hearts become comfortable, we often turn away from God and loath restrictions on our behavior by the law. By our own strength, we are unable to obey all that the law commands. The experience of the Jews is a realistic depiction: despite our covenant with God, we fail again and again to keep it. Therefore, Hebrews 8 clearly explains, "For if that first covenant had been faultless, there would have been no need to look for a second one. God finds fault with them when he says: 'The days are surely coming, says the Lord, when I will establish a new covenant with the house of Israel and with the house of Judah; not like the covenant that I made with their ancestors, on the day when I took them by the hand to lead them out of the land of Egypt; for they did not continue in my covenant, and so I had no concern for them', says the Lord." (Hebrews 8:7-9) The new covenant mentioned in the book of Hebrews had already been declared through the prophet Jeremiah more than 100 years prior to Nehemiah's time, "But this is the covenant that I will make with the house of Israel after those days, says the Lord: I will put my law within them, and I will write it on their hearts; and I will be their God, and they shall be my people. No longer shall they teach one another, or say to each other, 'Know the Lord,' for they shall all know me, from the least of them to the greatest, says the Lord; for I will forgive their iniquity, and remember their sin no more." (Jeremiah 31:33-34) This new covenant pre-ordained by God Himself was finally fulfilled in Jesus Christ.

Jesus Christ is God Most High. Descending from heaven, the Word became flesh; Jesus became fully human just like you and me. He was fully human in body and temperament. He encountered temptations and sufferings, but he overcame all of them and obeyed God's will perfectly, to the point of being crucified on the cross for our sin. The Bible tells us, "who, though he was in the form of God, did not regard equality with God as something to be exploited, but emptied himself, taking the form of a slave, being born in human likeness. And being found in human form, he humbled himself and became obedient to the point of death—even death on a cross." (Philippians 2:6-8) Perfectly sinless, holy, and just, Jesus Christ, who was born in human likeness, became the high priest who sacrificed for the sin of all people. The sacrifice He offered was no longer the bulls or rams commanded by the Law of Moses, but His own blood and body, by which He established a covenant with each one of us who repent and believe. Hebrews 9 clearly explained, "But when Christ came as a high priest of the good things that have come, then through the greater and perfect tent (not made with hands, that is, not of this creation), he entered once for all into the Holy Place, not with the blood of goats and calves, but with his own blood, thus obtaining eternal redemption." (Hebrews 9:11-12)

The sacrifice people offered according to the Law of Moses, "deal only with food and drink and various baptisms, regulations for the body imposed until the time comes to set things right." (Hebrews 9:10) The rituals God established through Moses were a shadow of the real sacrifice to be accomplished by Jesus. (Hebrews 8:5) Because of the grace of God, Christians today do not live under the Old Testament laws, but live in the new covenant that Jesus Christ established with us by his blood and body. This new covenant was the one Jeremiah prophesied about, that God "will put my [God's] law within them, and I [God] will write it on their hearts." (Jeremiah 31:33)

Even though our outward behavior is no longer bound by Old Testament laws, Jesus clearly told us, "Do not think that I have come to abolish the law or the prophets; I have come not to abolish but to fulfill. For truly I tell you, until heaven and earth pass away, not one letter, not one stroke of a letter, will pass from the law until all is accomplished." (Matthew 5:17-18) God's people no longer live under the Law today, because Jesus Christ has fulfilled all holy and just requirements of the Old Testament. Therefore, we are equipped to live out the true spirit of the Law—to love God and to love others, and make ourselves a blessing to others, and share the good news of the salvation of Jesus Christ wherever we are.

# Lesson 7: Back to Jerusalem, the Second Reform

### Suggested answers for your reference:

## ❖Fill in the blanks❖

(1) When Nehemiah returned back to Jerusalem for the sec-

ond time, he realized the people had abandoned their covenant with the Lord in four areas: 1) the priests abused their power; 2) tithing stopped; 3) the Sabbath was not observed; 4) the Jews intermarried with foreign women.

(2) On that day they read from the book of Moses in the hearing of the people; and in it was found written that no Ammonite or Moabite should ever enter the assembly of God, because they did not meet the Israelites with bread and water, but hired Balaam against them to curse them—yet our God turned the curse into a blessing. (Nehemiah 13:1-2)

(3) ...and returned to Jerusalem. I then discovered the wrong that Eliashib had done on behalf of Tobiah, preparing a room for him in the courts of the house of God. And I was very angry, and I threw all the household furniture of Tobiah out of the room. Then I gave orders and they cleansed the chambers, and I brought back the vessels of the house of God, with the grain offering and the frankincense. (Nehemiah 13:7-9)

(4) Remember this also in my favor, O my God, and spare me according to the greatness of your steadfast love. (Nehemiah 13:22)

## ❖Scripture Study❖

(1) Please find the passage in Deuteronomy chapter 23, where it was written that, "no Ammonite or Moabite should ever

enter the assembly of God." (Nehemiah 13:1)

Suggested answer: Ammonites and Moabites were the descendants of Abraham's nephew Lot, conceived by Lot's two daughters after they made their father drunk and laid with him. When the Israelites came out of Egypt, "Moab was in great dread of the people, because they were so numerous; Moab was overcome with fear of the people of Israel." (Numbers 22:3) They went to the false prophet Balaam and bribed him to curse Israel. But God prevented Balaam from doing so. Later, Balaam schemed to entice Israelite men into sexual sin so that the Lord's anger was kindled against Israel. Therefore, in the Book of Deuteronomy, God commanded Israel through Moses, "No Ammonite or Moabite shall be admitted to the assembly of the Lord. Even to the tenth generation, none of their descendants shall be admitted to the assembly of the Lord, because they did not meet you with food and water on your journey out of Egypt, and because they hired against you Balaam son of Beor, from Pethor of Mesopotamia, to curse you. (Yet the Lord your God refused to heed Balaam; the Lord your God turned the curse into a blessing for you, because the Lord your God loved you.) You shall never promote their welfare or their prosperity as long as you live." (Deut. 23:3-6)

(2) Why did Nehemiah chase one of the grandsons of Eliashib

out of the province of Judah?

Suggested answer: Leviticus 21:14 commanded that a high priest could only marry "a virgin of his own kin." In his prayer, Nehemiah mentioned his reason for chasing one of the grandsons of Eliashib out of the province of Judah was "because they have defiled the priesthood, the covenant of the priests and the Levites." (Neh 13:29) Nehemiah did that in order to cleanse the Israelites from everything foreign that could lead them astray (Neh 13:30) and stop them from intermarrying with gentile women. He knew that God hated it when Israelites, especially the priests, married foreign women and thus worshiped their idols. The prophet Malachi, who served at around the same time as Nehemiah, also proclaimed God's judgment, saying, "Judah has been faithless, and abomination has been committed in Israel and in Jerusalem; for Judah has profaned the sanctuary of the Lord, which he loves, and has married the daughter of a foreign god. May the Lord cut off from the tents of Jacob anyone who does this—any to witness or answer, or to bring an offering to the Lord of hosts." (Malachi 2:11-12)

(3) Please list Scripture from Jeremiah 17:27 and Ezekiel 20:23-24, where the prophets Jeremiah and Ezekiel warned the Israelites that if they did not keep the Sabbath day holy, Jerusalem would be ruined and they would be driven away

from their homeland.

Suggested answer: Jeremiah 17:27, "But if you do not listen to me, to keep the sabbath day holy, and to carry in no burden through the gates of Jerusalem on the sabbath day, then I will kindle a fire in its gates; it shall devour the palaces of Jerusalem and shall not be quenched."

Ezekiel 22:23-24, "Moreover I swore to them in the wilderness that I would scatter them among the nations and disperse them through the countries, because they had not executed my ordinances, but had rejected my statutes and profaned my sabbaths, and their eyes were set on their ancestors' idols."

## ❖Discussion and sharing❖

(1) Nehemiah "threw all the household furniture of Tobiah out of the room. Then I gave orders and they cleansed the chambers." (Nehemiah 13:8-9) Did his behavior contradict the biblical teaching to "love your enemies and pray for those who persecute you" (Matthew 5:44)?

Suggested answer: Jesus taught in the Beatitudes to "love your enemies and pray for those who persecute you." (Matthew 5:44) Jesus said if we only loved those who loved us, cared about those who were friendly to us, we were like the unbelievers, presenting no testimony of love and forgiveness. "For he (Heavenly Father) makes his sun rise on the evil and on the good, and sends rain on the righteous and on the unrighteous." (Matthew 5:45) Therefore, if we want to be true children of God, we ought to forgive other people's transgressions against us. Even when they attack, hurt, falsely accuse us out of their evil and selfish ambition, we should still view them with the Heavenly Father's kindness, and pray for them so that they would repent and receive God's blessings. We ought always to remember that while we were still sinners, God, in his grace, saved us through the salvation that came through Jesus Christ.

The principle of love and blessing does not contradict Nehemiah's action when he "threw all the household furniture of Tobiah out of the room." This is because what Nehemiah did was not an act of revenge out of the lack of forgiveness for personal loss. His intention was to prevent the returnees from further spiritual backsliding. His motivation was to cleanse the holy temple and to restore its function as a place for worship and sacrifices. Not allowing Tobiah to stay in the storehouse of the Temple was Nehemiah's act of obedience to the teaching of the Torah. Only when Tobiah was driven out could the storeroom be restored to its former function and the abuse of Eliashib and the officials be corrected.

Nehemiah's motivation, stance, and action in dealing with this issue parallels that of Jesus when he cleansed the Temple. The Bible tells us, "The Passover of the Jews was near, and Jesus went up to Jerusalem. In the temple he found people selling cattle, sheep, and doves, and the money changers seated at their tables. Making a whip of cords, he drove all of them out of the temple, both the sheep and the cattle. He also poured out the coins of the money changers and overturned their tables. He told those who were selling the doves, "Take these things out of here! Stop making my Father's house a marketplace!'" (John 2:13-16) "Zeal for your house will consume me" was how Jesus felt when he cleansed the Temple. Such was Nehemiah's principle when he dealt with the issue relating to Tobiah.

(2) Do you think Nehemiah matches Jesus' description of a "faithful and wise slave" in Matthew 24:45-46?

Suggested answer: During his first term as governor, Nehemiah rebuilt the broken walls of Jerusalem, restored sacrifices in the Temple, restored tithing, and established the duties of the Temple servants. When he returned to Jerusalem for his second term, he again upheld the regulations in the Temple and settled the Temple servants back in. Nehemiah found that the officials and Eliashib, who were in charge of the storehouse, had abused their power and did not distribute the tithes of wine and oil to the priest, the Levites, singers and gatekeepers at the appointed times. As the Temple servants stopped receiving their portions for livelihood, they were forced to go back to their fields to make a living.

In response, Nehemiah set out to cleanse the storehouses of the Temple by appointing faithful and righteous officials over them so that the people's tithe could be properly stored and Temple workers could have rooms to live in. Nehemiah also instracted people to give wood offerings at appointed times so as to keep the fire on the altar burning. Nehemiah "established the duties of the priests and Levites, each in his work," (Nehemiah 13:30) so that singers and gatekeepers could serve in the Temple as usual, and the priests and the Levites could minister sacrifices for the people. Consequently, faith could again be integrated into people's daily lives, and the Temple could be restored to being the center of worship.

In Matthew 24:45, Jesus asked, "Who then is the faithful and wise slave, whom his master has put in charge of his household, to give the other slaves their allowance of food at the proper time?" We can see Nehemiah as indeed a faithful and wise slave. We can also be sure that what Nehemiah did would please the Lord, because of what Jesus said next: "Blessed is that slave whom his master will find at work when he arrives." (Matthew 24:46) On the contrary, Eliashib was like the slave described in Matthew 24:48-51, "that wicked slave says to himself, 'My master is delayed,' and he begins to beat his fellow slaves, and eats and drinks with drunkards, the master of that slave will come on a day when he does not expect him and at an hour that he does not know. He will cut him in to pieces and put him among the hypocrites, where there will be weeping and gnashing of teeth."

(3) Nehemiah's final prayer in the book of Nehemiah was, "Remember me, O my God, for good" (Neh 13:31). Have you ever prayed a similar prayer? If so, under what circumstances did you pray?

Suggested answer: A free discussion among the students is encouraged. The teacher shall remind students that this prayer – "Remember me, O my God, for good," (Neh 13:31) is a frequently repeated theme in the whole book. Nehemiah lifted up the same prayer in 5:19, 13:14, 22 & 31. Nehemiah did not seek honor and praise from others. Rather, his heart was dedicated to please and serve God. He asked God to remember him. Nehemiah's focus throughout his ministry was to lead the returnees to walk in the teachings of the Torah and reestablish their holy relationship with God. Like the Apostle Paul, Nehemiah sought reward from God alone. He was truly a great model for every Christ follower.

# In conclusion

Jeremiah once prophesied, "Is Ephraim my dear son? Is he the child I delight in? As often as I speak against him, I still remember him. Therefore I am deeply moved for him; I will surely have mercy on him, says the Lord." (Jeremiah 31:20) Whereas Nehemiah seemed harsh when he rebuked those who did wrong, his relentless efforts were all for the good of the people. Toward the end of the Book of Nehemiah, Nehemiah's final prayer, a cry that he often uttered, could be heard loudly: "Remember me, O my God, for good." (Neh 13:31) Nehemiah did not desire to be praised or repaid by the people; he asked only that God would remember everything he did for the holy city, the Temple, and God's people. His vigor and strictness might have brought on himself much resistance, yet he chose to be faithful to the God-given mission and dedicated his all to restoring godly living among God's chosen people as they returned to Judah. Nehemiah's uncompromising faith and unrelenting courage are truly admirable.

Nehemiah's background and education differed from that of Ezra. Their personality and style also differed. Yet, they clearly shared a common trait: both leaders valued the word of God, and obeyed God's regulations and precepts in words and in action. When dealing with the issues among the Jews, Nehemiah was harsh and Ezra was soft, but neither of them was afraid of the power of men, nor did they try to appease authority or tolerate corruption. When it came to being faithful to God's calling, they both showed a determination to please God alone. They toiled and struggled with all of their might for the house of God, in order to put the returnees back on track spiritually.

Today, after more than 2,000 years of being without a nation, the Jews not only did not get assimilated into other nations and disappear completely, but they have kept their faith and culture. They reestablished the nation Israel in 1948, which was indeed a miracle from God. The contributions of Nehemiah and Ezra made them precious vessels and faithful servants in the household of God. They worked with God and became great men of God in history. As us conclude our study of Ezra and Nehemiah, may we all treasure the teachings of the Bible and follow them wholeheartedly, as what Ezra and Nehemiah did in their time.

# Appendix

Spring of Water International Ministry
Multimedia Bible Learning Material
Instruction for Bible Study Group Leaders
and Instructors

The term "the group leader" below is referred to anyone who is leading the Bible study group or the instructor who is conducing the teaching session in a classroom.

## The Bible Study Process using SOW Bible Study Set (SBSS)

Following an "open learning" principle and the Bible study course schedule, SBSS allows 50-120 minutes for each lesson of the study guide. Every lesson has three stages: Preparation, Development, and Conclusion, with the allocated duration of 5-15 minutes, 40-90 minutes, and 5-15 minutes, respectively. The group leader can adjust the time periods and course content to fit the needs of the situation. SBSS can also be adopted in a classroom Bible-teaching process. Each stage is described in detail below:

##  A. Preparation (5-15 minutes):

The purpose of this stage is to help the Bible study group members warm up, lead them into the theme of the lesson, and spark their interest in learning. Depending on the time available and the occasion, the group leader can conduct any of the following activities:

**1. Icebreaker:** While waiting for late arrivals, ice-breaker activities can be conducted in any of the following ways:

    a.  Introduce new comers.

    b.  Greet one another by asking a question.

    c.  Share what is happening around each person, or any application from the previous lesson, or any development on things that we are praying through in our intercessory prayers.

    d.  Discuss the latest news or events of interest to all.

    e.  Play a game related to the subject of the study of the day.

**2. Introduction:** Introduce the subject of the lesson and provide a mental sketch for the direction of the study. It can be conducted in one of the following ways:

    a. Introduce the goals of the lesson.

    b. Present the outline of the lesson.

    c. Sum up what was taught in the previous lesson, then begin the subject of the lesson.

    d. Ask a question that is relevant to the lesson of the day and allow the group members to answer, then proceed into the subject.

**3. Opening Prayer:** Before going into the subject of the lesson, pray and read the Scriptures to prepare members' hearts to learn and be humble.

Pray for the presence of the Holy Spirit that will anoint the words of the group leader, and open the hearts of the group members, to let in Christ Jesus' living water to nurture and enrich everyone.

## B. Development (40-90 minutes):

This stage is where the main activities of the Bible study are organized. The focus is to have group members assimilate new learning into their existing cognitive system effectively through a multifaceted and fun-filled process.

The group leader can conduct the Development stage in the following manner:

**1. Scripture Reading:** Everyone takes turns reading aloud or in silence the portion of the Scriptures as described in the course schedule, to establish the outline.

**2. Synopsis:** The group leader gives a brief summary of 3 to 10 minutes on the text. Alternatively questions and answers in Scripture study can be used to bring out the main points and help group members to recall, digest, and consolidate what they had learned.

**3. Video Viewing:** Play the video clip as suggested for the lesson. Most sessions will last about 5 to 10 minutes. Make sure to have a suitable environment by keeping things such as light, volume, and noise in check.

**4. Study Questions:** Group participation is essential during this phase. The group leader leads the Bible study group members to discuss, share, or apply biblical principles that are within the scope of the lesson. During this activity, interaction among group members should take up most of the time, and the group leader should stay in the role of a facilitator. It is recommended for the group leader not take up over to exceed 30% of the total discussion time. At the end, the group leader moves onto the next phase of concluding the discussion, moderating sharing, and suggesting applications from the lesson.

##  C. Conclusion (5-15 minutes):

The purpose is to consolidate the lessons learned through the study, and lead the group members to apply them in their daily lives.

**1. Summary:** At the end of each study, the group leader gives a review of what has been learned, to make sure each group member has clear understanding of the Scripture and reaches the goals of the lesson. It can be conducted in any of the following ways:

    a. Review the lesson.

    b. Assess the effectiveness of the study through questions and answers.

    c. Apply today's lesson and anticipate future learning.

    d. Read aloud together the **key** Bible verses

related to the study.

   e.   Encourage group members to practice what they just learned in their daily living.

**2. Closing Prayer:** For a large group, the group leader can be the one who prays for the whole group and conclude the study. For a smaller group, it can be done through intercessory prayer among the group members. Praying for each other is not only a spiritual practice, but it also develops and grows relationships among group members.

SBSS uses multimedia materials as a platform and allows Bible study group leaders to facilitate of discussion and sharing. The following table is a lesson plan for using SBSS to lead a Bible study group. It can also be adopted in a Bible teaching classroom for the Bible teaching instructors.

## The Procedures of the Multimedia Bible Study Set

### I. Preparation (5-15 minutes)

| | |
|---|---|
| 1 | Icebreaker/ Introduction |
| 2 | Opening Prayer |

### II. Development (40-90 minutes)

| | |
|---|---|
| 1 | Scripture Reading |
| 2 | Synopsis |
| 3 | Video Viewing |
| 4 | Study Questions |

### III. Conclusion (5-15 minutes)

| | |
|---|---|
| 1 | Summary, Homework Assignment |
| 2 | Closing Prayer |